A438

A SEAL UPON MY HEART

A Seal
Upon My Heart

Autobiographies of Twenty Sisters

EDITED BY

GEORGE L. KANE

THE BRUCE PUBLISHING COMPANY
MILWAUKEE

NIHIL OBSTAT:

    JOHN A. SCHULIEN, S.T.D.
    Censor librorum

IMPRIMATUR:

    ✠ ALBERTUS G. MEYER
    Archiepiscopus Milwauchiensis
    October 25, 1956

Rosary College Dewey Classification Number: 271.9
Library of Congress Catalog Card Number: 57–6658

© 1957 BY THE BRUCE PUBLISHING COMPANY
MADE IN THE UNITED STATES OF AMERICA

INTRODUCTION

IN THIS book you will meet twenty very different religious women. There are over half a million more scattered around the globe, and one hundred and fifty-nine thousand, five hundred and forty-five of them can be found in North America. Each of them has her own way of loving and serving God. But all of them have one thing in common. They are called "sisters," and their lives are dedicated wholly to Christ as members of a religious community.

How did they become sisters? The answer is here for you to find. In the following autobiographies each one of these women has put down the story of her choice of the religious life. She tells about her vocation and how the call was answered. One heard Christ while serving with the New York Division of Parole; another heard Him on the beach at Waikiki.

One sister tells how she lost her faith while attending college, but regained it during graduate work in psychology at a secular university. Still another relates the unique experience of leaving a community of Anglican nuns, becoming a Catholic, and entering a Benedictine convent — all on the same day.

The stories are varied. But running through each of them is an awareness of God and His meaning in their life. Some found Him in visits to the Blessed Sacrament and frequent Holy Communion. Others were drawn closer to Christ by family devotion, like saying the rosary or kneeling together for night prayers. Still others found Him in the dusty tomes on a library shelf, while their companions learned about Him from the pages of a little pamphlet on convent life.

These autobiographies reveal the many-faceted workings of divine grace in a human soul. They tell how each of these sisters gradually discovers that the things of this world — popularity, beauty, clothes, comfort, and success — are not nearly so important as peace of mind and security in the love of God. They let us glimpse that moment of awareness when the girl learns that there is only one way she can become absolutely happy, and she goes boldly ahead with her application for admittance to the convent. They arouse our sympathy for family and friends who are saddened at her leaving, and with the loved ones we try to plumb the meaning of that remark with which she — like most religious women — sums up her vocation: "I've fallen head over heels in love with Christ. That's why I want to be a sister."

As each story repeats this theme, we recall what we have seen of this phenomenon before. A girl falls in love with a boy and her life is changed. Suddenly she has found the prince for whom she has been waiting. Going for a walk or to a movie, which used to be only mildly interesting to her, now becomes a high adventure.

Perhaps we wonder at this transformation, and as opportunity offers we try to question her. But the answers are often as unintelligible as the one sister gave. For the girl in love is content with her beloved's company and wants merely to be with him. Sometimes she may not even speak, for her thoughts have leapt beyond words. She is in love.

No other explanation is necessary. No other is possible.

Now something of this same realization comes over one, while reading this remarkable book, compiled by Father George L. Kane, Director of Religious Education for the Diocese of Antigonish, Nova Scotia. There is a transformation in the life of every girl who becomes a sister. When she enters religious life she is so much in love with God that the Church in the liturgy calls her a "bride of Christ."

Earlier this girl has considered all the things in the world which she can do. She recognizes that she has talents and abilities for many professions. She has the blessings of health and a good head on her shoulders. But most important of all she shows in her eyes an innocence of heart and a purity of soul. What a wonderful wife and mother she would make! What a brilliant career she could have!

Then as this girl talks the matter over with her confessor, we see how she is beginning to weigh the various opportunities. Something seems to be wanting. Each work or profession seems to her incomplete. She cannot give herself absolutely generously to the things of this world. When at length she turns to the religious life, it is because she has found that to be the best way to love and serve God. Only the sisterhood challenges her fullest generosity. Only as a "bride of Christ" can she be completely happy.

These ideas are not mere figures of speech or poetic expressions. They are realities. For in the beautifully impressive ritual of Reception most communities dress the girl in a bridal gown. She then comes up the aisle of the convent chapel and kneels before God's representative at the altar. There she pledges her heart, mind, and whole being irrevocably to Christ. Henceforth she belongs entirely to Him and wears His ring.

The only hard part of all this is that sister does not see her Beloved face to face. She lives under the same roof with Him, and each morning receives Him in Holy Communion. Many times during the day she stops in the chapel to visit with Him and discuss her work. But faith alone assures her of His presence and closeness. It will not be until the eyes of her soul are opened in death that she will see Him as He is. Then in a blinding flash of glory she will be swept into the joys of the Beatific Vision.

Yet in anticipation of that great day these twenty sisters — like their thousands of companions — are working hard at their appointed tasks. Sometimes the work becomes monotonous, and often there is little to buoy them up except the consciousness that they are pleasing God every moment of their life and doing all that is possible with their time. Such knowledge keeps them happy and faithful. This is also the secret of why there is so much joy and gaiety in their convents — why sisters seem to be brimming over with zeal and enthusiasm for the things of God.

Personally I am grateful to Father Kane for assembling this wonderful group of religious women and letting me introduce them. And I marvel that he has prevailed upon them to tell so much. But in this he will help Catholics everywhere appreciate more the life and work of sisters. He will also afford encouragement to those girls who may themselves be called to such a life.

May then all read and ponder the lessons of this book. Too often I am asked: "Why are there not more sisters?" The reason is obvious. Many of our girls and women who are qualified have not taken the time to consider the truths revealed here. Many more have not prayed for the generosity to give themselves completely to Christ. For if they reflected and prayed, thousands would leave what this world offers for a life in the convent. They would recognize the promptings of grace and exclaim: "If these twenty sisters can do it, so can I!"

REVEREND GODFREY POAGE, C.P.

PREFACE

THE sustained and almost universal popularity of the mystery story in the twentieth century is symptomatic of modern man's intense curiosity. Mystery intrigues him, and he seeks to know the explanation. While there is a special fascination in arriving at the solution on his own, he is willing to be shown, if necessary, provided the whole mystery is unraveled and all the riddle solved. Certainly, the most unsatisfactory sort of mystery is one that is never cleared up, and the mystery story that leaves the reader in doubt about the solution is frustrating to a high degree.

But there are other mysteries besides those between the covers of books that intrigue the modern mind. There is mystery in the doctor's consulting room, in the hospital operating room, backstage in the theater, in the copyroom of a metropolitan newspaper; indeed, whatever is unfamiliar is an unfailing source of mystery. If familiarity breeds contempt, unfamiliarity generates curiosity.

Perhaps no place is more suggestive of mystery to many a modern than a Catholic convent, and no person takes up a more baffling way of life than the Catholic nun. She is a sort of living mystery in herself, not in the sense of a whodunit but in the sense of whydidshedoit. Of course, there are those who have completely solved the mystery to their own satisfaction, and the case is closed. The nun is merely suffering from a severe neurosis; or she is the victim of faulty education; or she has a morbid fear of hell; or, most commonly, she has been disappointed in love and has fled the world.

But these are the solutions reached without a study of the

clues or an examination of the evidence and are based on prejudice, bigotry, or lack of information, or a combination of all three. Those moderns who have had any contact with Catholic nuns have made the rather surprising and certainly refreshing discovery that nuns are very normal women and that their lives are exceptionally happy; that they differ as much from one another as people in any other class or group; and that one looks in vain for a specific "convent type." And these very facts intensify the mystery and make more insistent the demand for an answer to the question: Why?

No nun can give a completely satisfactory answer to the question, even to herself. We might almost say especially to herself, for she is perhaps more mystified than anyone else. The reason is that she knows only part of the answer; the other part is God's and He's not telling. In other words, the mystery of a vocation to religious life is partly human and partly divine, and the divine part cannot be told this side of heaven.

But the human part can be related in full, and in each of the twenty cases presented in this collection the author, acting as her own private eye, uncovers sufficient evidence and provides enough clues to enable the reader to understand, if not to solve, the mystery. In any case, it is a mystery of fact, not of fiction.

The editor wishes to express his gratitude to the authors for their gracious co-operation in preparing this book, and for the candor and human interest which make their autobiographies so readable and vibrant. To Father Godfrey Poage, C.P., the editor was already indebted for many kindnesses, and the splendid Introduction to this volume has greatly increased a debt that can never be adequately paid.

REV. GEORGE L. KANE

North Sydney, Nova Scotia
October 17, 1956

CONTENTS

CONTENTS

A SEAL UPON MY HEART

WE SOUND SO YOUNG

SISTER MARY CECILY, S.L.[1]

WE SAT in the back of the taxi, nudged each other, and laughed. The cab driver had just said, "Say, you two sound rather young. I've never known any nuns, but I thought they were all up in the sixties or seventies."

Sister Helen Jean and I were riding out to our convent from Union Station about 11:30 one night, having just got off the train from Chicago, where earlier that day we had administered some scholarship exams. It was late. We had talked all afternoon on the train, with time out for prayers and spiritual reading, and I suppose we were just watching the Saturday night traffic and thinking about the joy of getting home again. Coming out the Superhighway past Forest Park, we were remarking in a small-talk way about the yellow safety lights and cleverly blinking neon signs. And that occasioned the driver's comment.

---

[1] *Sister Mary Cecily is a native of East St. Louis, Illinois. After being graduated from college she became a Sister of Loretto at the Foot of the Cross. She now teaches English at Webster College, Webster Groves 19, Missouri. Since this sketch was written, she has been appointed dean of students at the College. Her community, whose mother house is at Nerinx P. O., Loretto, Kentucky, is engaged in teaching at all levels, elementary, high school, and college, and in giving spiritual and temporal assistance to the poor and the sick.*

We laughed, but not at the fact that he thought us young. Most people do. Nuns are quite accustomed to the utter inability of people to guess their ages, often being accused of fooling the public by looking ten or twenty years younger than their lay contemporaries. We were laughing at the driver's complete dismay over the fact that we could be young — or sound young — and still be nuns.

We assured him that nuns all start out relatively young in years (I'd say at eighteen to thirty, though a few enter a bit earlier and a few a bit later) and that being young in heart was a kind of religious hallmark.

He digested that for a few moments in silence. But as we were approaching Clayton (two suburbs from Webster and only fifteen minutes from home), he began fishing for information again. He was not quite sure how to phrase his next query, and so he fumbled with, "How long does it take . . . I mean, how long do you study to be nuns?"

That having been satisfactorily answered by Sister Helen Jean, he had one more: "Tell me, don't you ever want to . . . well, kick over the traces? I mean, it seems to me that if I were a girl, I'd want to hang up that black dress you wear and put on a party dress some night and have a good time."

This question couldn't be so briefly answered as those that concern, "How long?" "How old?" "What kind of clothes?" The lad was hunting for a capsule treatment on the motives for a girl's becoming a nun and on the essence of religious life itself. I knew Sister Helen Jean could put him straight, and so I left the job to her.

It was late; I was tired. Listening to Sister Helen Jean's even, assured, and — yes, young-sounding — voice was soothing, a bit too soothing. . . . Yet I caught snatches of the conversation. . . . "Gave up that kind of good time. . . . But it's missing the point to think of it as a negative giving up. . . . If it were just that, we'd be a bunch of disgruntled women. . . . We've given up some things, and things that are good, but we've been given so much more. . . . Being in love with God is a positive thing. . . . Nuns are the happiest people in the world. . . ."

I could hear the come and go of his questions, the shy delving to locate the causes that make us the way we are. I knew we were becoming less and less a mystery to a man who had, apparently, never before happened to get a speaking acquaintance with a sister.

Though quite drowsy, I was thinking, thinking along the same line, but thinking of one nun only. I was thinking of me! Now we were passing through Clayton, and I saw the crowded parking lot at Medart's, still one of the most popular places for teen-agers and the college crowd. That brought back memories of the times we'd gone there after games and shows and parties at school. It isn't too hard to remember back seven or eight years, and the fact that I am now stationed at the school where I had been a college girl makes the remembering easier. The cab driver was probing and was being answered. I was probing my own mind and was being answered too. Why had I decided to hang up the party dresses and wear a black one for life?

Most girls who have gone through the usual grade-school, high-school pattern of Catholic education with sisters teaching them, have probably decided at one time or another — perhaps in a moment of heroine worship or, I like to think, perhaps in an inspired moment of pure generosity to God, a moment that He often repeats in their more mature years — that they would like to become sisters. For me that moment came when I was in the fourth grade. We entered an essay contest that term, and I scrawled a contribution on the subject, "What I Hope To Be and Why." I hoped to be a nun. The years from fourth year grammar school to fourth year college stretch out long, with much between, and the story of "What I Hope To Be and Why" seemed to be marked "continued later . . . much later."

And yet I have a notion that I really did think about religious life between times, for I can remember with an embarrassed smile how, during the annual retreat we made in high school and college, I used to pray that the retreat master wouldn't give a talk on vocations. Marriage was all right, single blessedness, too, but not religious vocations. Maybe I was afraid I had one. Invariably, of course, there would be a conference on religious life. I used to squirm. Retreat, however, lasted only three days, and I could forget about that one talk. Besides, I didn't have to decide anything yet. This put-off-the-decision technique worked perfectly until my last year in college. After all, when a girl is twenty-one, it's pretty silly for her not to face things, especially things like her own future.

One of my reasons for going to college was that I really wanted to become a professional writer. I majored in English, but somewhere along the line Mom suggested that it would be a good idea for me to take a few courses in teacher training so that I'd really have something to do after graduation. Mom, you see, is a practical woman, and she couldn't agree to having her only daughter up in an attic, even her own attic, starving while she worked on the great American novel. I wasn't keen on teaching school. In fact, I was quite reluctant, convinced that you shouldn't teach unless you liked to, yet wondering at the same time how you could know about liking it if you didn't try.

So, sandwiched into the middle of my senior year along with coediting the paper, keeping up my club activities, preparing lots of classwork, and enjoying every moment of our social life, I had about four weeks of practice teaching in a journalism class of high school juniors. This was fun. These were people. They were learning. We put out a mimeographed class paper. They glowed in the effervescent way high schoolers do. I glowed inside. I was excited, more excited than I could have been over selling a story. Something had been sold to me.

Maybe I would teach school — and write books on the side, I added to myself! Maybe I would teach school . . . maybe I would teach school . . . maybe this was the way I was supposed to know the answer. But you could be a school teacher without being a nun. You could teach school for a while, and then. . . .

That year I had been doing a lot of thinking, even before the practice-teaching development. Ours was — and is — a relatively small girls' school, a homey place where one could come to know the nuns with more than a "Good morning, Sister" relationship. (The cab was skimming through Maplewood now, taking the curves of the Big Bend Road swiftly and easily.) I was remembering many of these nuns, some with whom I am now living in community, and some who have been transferred to other schools staffed by our Congregation. There was the tall, spare Dean of Women, with a witty tongue and an understanding heart; she had been a dancer, they said. There were the two who taught me English. I was remembering the nights we worked late on the paper, the fun we used to have at English Club, the time the staff went on a picnic and the two moderators had enjoyed it so much. There was the sparkling, swift one who has charge of the sacristy and the bookstore; no alumna from the past fifteen years ever returns without asking first for her. There was my French teacher, older than those, with a teasable Kentucky accent and laughing blue eyes. There was the stout one who ran the cafeteria and who spoils me now because she knows I like doughnuts.

I had come to know them well, and now I know that knowing them was what set me to thinking about becoming one of them. They were individuals. Each had a completely different background, education, duties. Two things they all were: happy and young in spirit. They were human: they laughed a lot, they teased one another, they almost bubbled over with happiness. They were prayerful. I don't think I ever ducked into the college chapel for a visit — and there were lots of "ducks" during that year of decision — without seeing several of them there between the times for regular community prayers. They were easily familiar with God, and it was just as natural for a sister to take you by the hand and say, "Let's go in and say 'Hi' to God," as it was for her to red-pencil the assignments you wrote or ask about the date of the night before. They were gay with the gaiety that grows from being genuinely and generously in love with God and from getting a terrific "charge," as the freshmen used to say, out of their work.

Those chapel sessions that year would usually end with a reluctant acquiescence, for I did not realize what a gilt-edged invitation I was getting. I was too much I. Yet God was inviting me to a lifetime (and a forever-after time) of happiness that I don't know the right words for! I'd find myself praying . . . I do want to do it if You want me to . . . But I am not sure . . . O.K., Lord . . . I'll go . . . I'll go soon.

It was always *soon*, but never *now*, until finally I decided something. I decided to wait a year — just to make sure, I said. That decision came on the day I was graduated, and the way I rationalized it out to God, for at the time He was the only one who knew, was something like this: I loved Webster. I loved everything about it — our traditions, our teachers, our class, Mary See and Pat and Mary Grace and Marg, the fun we had had. Maybe I was mistaking loving a school for . . . you know, things can get mixed up inside. And a girl's heart is a girl's heart. If I were going to the convent, I wanted to go with an intellectual conviction that God wanted me to go. I didn't care about sentiment. I didn't want the sentiment. That's why I told God I'd wait, thank You.

I waited. The next year I took a couple of courses at the university here, and I did some part-time teaching. I also had a part-time proofreading-typing job at a Catholic publishing house, which was the closest I'd been to "the ink" yet. I used to debate the relative merits of teaching and correcting somebody else's copy. The former always won, for I genuinely loved it. But I suppose I wasn't really debating between teaching and anything else. I was wriggling around looking for a decision.

The straight fact was that I was waiting for the courage and the generosity to say yes. But I soon found out that it was God who was the generous one in giving me a vocation. When you're trying to decide, though, you're likely to go through a lot of heroics! Finally I thought to myself, "You like to put things down on paper. Why don't you just list your reasons, for and against, pro and con?" I did. The pro's won.

There wasn't anything ultraheroic about the actual going, nor anything dramatic. I remember hating to shop for ugly black oxfords. It was June and I kept looking at my red play shoes. I remember reading a slick magazine on the train going to the novitiate. I remember the twangy voice of the conductor calling our stop and the knowing way in which he eyed our black suitcases as the three of us alighted. But it was all quite customary.

I did get homesick, but that's just one of the sacrifices. I've not started that great American novel, and I shall probably not do so very soon! But I've done some writing. In the convent any ability, even knowing how to one-finger your way up and down a piano keyboard, is used. I've "given up" some things, but in the bargain with God in which a nun gives her all, she receives all — multiplied according to God's arithmetic.

Yes, I've grown quite accustomed to black stockings. I've even learned to darn them. (The cab was in Old Orchard now, almost home.) Wiggling my toes inside my best pair of shoes, I could feel the crisscross of tiny stitches I had needled into the hole that had appeared in the left stocking just before packing for the Chicago trip.

We were turning slightly as we came to the bend in the road before entering Lockwood Avenue. There to the left, dark against the moonlight, I could see the outlines of the high school where I had done that stretch of practice teaching. I knew I hadn't become a nun because I like to teach school. You can teach, and do it well, as Miss Anybody.

I had gone to the novitiate because I knew, as far as a girl can know without a knocking-her-off-a-horse bolt of lightning, that God wants me to love Him all the way. And it was pretty nice of Him to throw in the natural helps — liking the work I'd be doing for a good span of time, the various obvious happiness of the nuns I had known — along with the supernatural "Will you?"

I could hear Sister Helen Jean telling the driver that the entrance was just on this side of the mailbox there, and I could feel the swerve of the car as it nosed its way into the driveway. We were reaching for our briefcases. I knew how it would be to get out and run up the steps of the girls' residence, for the administration building would be locked, and we'd have to go through the connecting colonnade to get to the cloister. Yes, I knew how it would be, for we'd done this before — last year and the year before. Sister Rose Maureen and Sister Francis Jane would be there waiting, and we'd go back to the green kitchen in the Hall and have hot chocolate because they would think we needed that to make us sleep.

Then there would be the soft-stepping walk over to the other building and to bed. We'd stop at the chapel, and fumble around the toes of the Sacred Heart statue in the hallway to find the key, for the door would have been locked since ten o'clock, the convent curfew hour. We would kneel briefly in the back of the chapel by the white marble holy water font, trying to see the tabernacle in the dark. And I knew I'd unconsciously turn toward "my aisle," the one I clean, and be glad that Sister John Patrice had offered to give it the Saturday brush-up for me.

We would go swiftly down the first-floor hall, past my classroom on the corner, and then up to the cloistered fourth floor. My roommate would have my bed turned down and my slippers out. And I knew that that night I'd be extra careful in hanging up the puzzling black habit which wasn't ever going to be traded for a party frock!

The driver was out, swinging open the taxi door and checking the meter. Then he tipped his hat with a "Thank you," and, almost as an embarrassed afterthought, he added, "You even look young."

We laughed again, and turned to go up the steps. We could hear the cab pulling away and we could see the two nuns coming to open the door for us. It felt good to be young; it felt very good.

STAR-DUST AND STAIR-DUST

SISTER REGINA AGNES, C.S.J.[1]

WHEN my brother was at the "kid-brother" stage, he used to delight in reminding me with many a gleeful comparison to status quo that as a baby I had to be bribed to eat. I remember the bribes. There was a cereal bowl from which the beloved face of Peter Rabbit would smile up at me after the last spoonful had been taken. There was a red glass straw through which I could watch the progress of my milk. There were also all kinds of promises of toys, lollipops, and movies and, best of all, there was the serial story told by my mother of a certain adventuresome princess who could be rescued from harm only as the last morsel of spinach disappeared. I remember, too, the gesture with which I would hold up my emptied plate to be thanked for the favor I had done my mother by eating. I marvel, looking back, at the patience of mother love and its ingenuity in self-sacrifice.

As a story this tells nothing about my vocation, but as a parable it tells everything. The comparison between God's love and parental love is an obvious one. God Himself was the first to make it. He told us that He would not forget us

---

[1] *Sister Regina Agnes, a native of Brooklyn, New York, is a member of the Congregation of St. Joseph of Brentwood, Long Island, New York, a teaching community. She is at present on the faculty of St. Martin of Tours School, Brooklyn, and resides at St. Martin of Tours Convent, 305 Weirfield Street, Brooklyn 21, New York.*

any more than a mother would forget her child; that He would shield us as a mother hen shields her chicks under her wing; that like the father of the prodigal, His joy is to forgive.

To come back to my own story, God, like my mother, coaxed and cajoled me into accepting the very best of His gifts, a religious vocation. Why? Because if He had presented it at its immensely true value, I wouldn't have comprehended any more than I would have understood a dissertation on food values at the age of four.

The thought of becoming a nun first became very pressing while I was at Mary Louis, our Academy in Jamaica, New York. I did not quite know just what a nun was. Oh, yes, I knew what many nuns were as people: they loved God; they worked hard; they were happy; they were very nice to one another and to us — so nice that it seemed natural to me that they should have found a way to the kind and gentle Christ whom I wanted to find. But what was a nun really? . . . Some-one who belonged to God in a special way . . . I knew that and that was about all. At this point, if I had been instructed to read a tome or two on the religious life, I might have added considerably to my knowledge, but probably would have been frightened away from all thought of the convent. I might have read that I could expect great peace, fewer obstacles to salvation, greater hopes of spiritual progress — graces invaluable to me as a mature religious. As a teen-ager they would have left me cold.

I don't think I am unique in having been led to a voca-tion by a vague, indefinable, even romantic attraction. There were the fishermen — Christ's personal appeal to them was so winning that their nets slid from their fingers unnoticed and their boats slipped out with the tide unheeded. They knew they were following Him, but not exactly where they were going or why. The glory to which He had destined them would have been incomprehensible to their earthy minds. Therefore, He didn't bother to tell them about it. The bitter suffering and martyr's death which they would one day embrace with joy would have frightened them, so He shielded them from the knowledge. He just said, "Come, follow Me," and they came, drawn by a divine power of personal persuasion. My vocation was like that, too. It was a Person, wondrously winning, who wanted me to come. Where, how, why — didn't seem too important, so long as it was to be with Him. A mother's love and God's love! How beautiful is a mother's condescension to the limitations of a human baby, on the one hand, and God's condescension to a human soul, in its spiritual infancy, on the other.

No one could deserve a religious vocation. Certainly, it is least deserved by those who can accept it only when it is disguised in romantic garb — but God, like mothers, measures His love and generosity by His own great goodness, not by our scant merits. He would rather lessen the dignity of the presentation of His gift than have the loved one do without it.

Spiritually a teen-age girl is an infant. God bases His appeal to her on that ground. Emotionally, she has a complete feminine nature and so He calls to her through that too. He wanders through the imagination, thorn-crowned and alone, until the yearning to comfort Him becomes irresistible. He becomes again the poor Babe in a cold stable whose own would not receive Him, or the weary, disappointed Christ watching sadly the retreating figure of the Rich Young Man. Of course, we have not heard His invitation, "Follow Me," in so many words, but we have heard Him unmistakably through these tugs at our womanly sympathies.

Again, He draws us through our sense of the beautiful: wind-whirled clouds in a burning blue sky, stars swinging breathlessly low out of their night, the baptismal innocence shining under a child's long lashes, the first crocus lifting its yellow head recklessly into a March wind. He is far more than the Author of Beauty: He is its quickening and its sustaining principle. He causes created beauty to sing out with a thousand tongues, "Follow Him!"

It might be thought that the greatest obstacle to a religious vocation, especially in women, would be the desire to be loved — but God uses this too. I remember making a high-school retreat at the Cenacle at Ronkonkome, Long Island. I had guarded against things getting too dull by dragging along two of my liveliest friends, well provided, like myself, with pickles and potato chips and one of Ellery Queen's "Who Dun Its." We couldn't have been especially model retreatants because I remember one serious little nun telling us that she had said a special rosary that we would learn how to make a better retreat. But away below the surface the grace of God was at work, and I was doing some pretty deep thinking about life and love, what love meant and especially, what it meant to be loved. There wasn't *a boy* but there were boys, very interesting creatures, and there was also Christ, about whom I couldn't quite decide. The priest was very wise. He knew he was speaking to adolescent girls most of whom had some interest in a vocation. He didn't say one word about the religious life itself — its advantages, its noble position in the Church. Instead he took for his theme, "No one will ever love you as I do. No one will ever love you as much as you want to be loved but Me." That told me all I wanted to know. I'm sure that ascetic little Jesuit knew that the real glory of the religious life is not in being loved but in its complete immolation of self for the One who is loved. Like God and like mothers he met us on our own level.

Of course, there is a long distance to be traveled between the first response to God's invitation through sensible attractions and the fullness of the love of Christ. This is the purpose of the novitiate — to help romance grow into love. There *is* a glamour in the veil. Even Hollywood has discovered that but you don't live a movie — you only watch it. Actually the glamorous veil of Reception Day soon becomes something that hangs rather passively down your back while you are very actively up to your elbows in dish water. If a girl doesn't really have a vocation, she is, at this point, glad to be reminded of the time-honored novitiate adage, "The door swings both ways!" — especially out — and out she goes. But not if a girl has entered on God's invitation, though He may have couched His offer in the simplest terms in accord with her limited understanding. For her, this is not the end of the venture but the beginning of a weaning process. Each little difficulty is an opening for God to ask, "You can do this for Me, can't you?" Each time she answers "Yes" she is one step nearer to a mature concept of a vocation, and God, I realize now, is infinitely solicitous that one is given the opportunity to exercise the maximum of generosity without once being tried beyond the activating power of His given grace.

Of course, nobody but God really knows why I am in the convent. It was all His idea. I am more grateful for it with every year but I often wonder why God didn't give Mary Jane a vocation — Mary Jane who spent many an hour before the Blessed Sacrament while I was having my nails manicured; or Alice who did all the housework for her mother on Saturdays while I was enjoying matinees; and why didn't God give Helen the grace to last through her novitiate training, Helen who was so used to self-sacrifice, while I, an only girl from a comfortable, indulgent family, somehow was given the help to come through. His disposal of His gifts is a lovely and very sacred mystery, not to be solved by any musings over why I became a nun.

But I can think of reasons which are *not* why I became a nun. Above all, I'm sure that it was not because I was "different." Many people have a suspicion that a nun, even in the cradle, is attired in veil and wimple instead of the traditional apparel — even people who should know better. I remember the day I went to buy my "sister" shoes. I forget the

circumstances, but somehow my mother had gone out ahead
of me. We were to meet at Barclay Street. She did not,
therefore, have her usual opportunity to supervise my costume. When we met she looked me over from head to toe and
groaned, "What will the salesman think when he sees those
shoes!" They were red, toeless sandals. She had never minded
my wearing them before but now, as a girl who would soon
be a nun, she, my own mother, thought that I should be
"different." The salesman might be scandalized to see that a
girl in red shoes could become a nun. Now, my mother had
nearly twenty years of direct evidence in proof that I was
not "different." If she could fall into the ancient fallacy that
nuns are somehow not ordinary women, we shall certainly
have to forgive less well-informed spectators. I don't know what
happened to those red shoes. I wish I could will them to any
little girl who might be tempted by the evil logic: "Nuns are
not ordinary girls. I am an ordinary girl. Therefore I cannot
be a nun."

I like religious life. It doesn't obliterate the universal truth
that life is a warfare — no — but I like, for example, to live
in a house whose center is Christ, with people striving for
the same goal, who, without ties of blood, like one another.
I like my three vows because, by them, I am bound to Christ
in three ways more than is the holiest married woman I know.
I like to teach His children because they were made to praise
Him unceasingly in eternity and I can help them to reach
Him. I like so many things that I didn't even know about back
in the days when I thought a nun's chief occupation was
star-dusting. To think God could be less than Absolute
Truth would be heresy. But I know only that He led me here
on an adolescent search for star-dust that turned out to be
merely stair-dust (and chair-dust and other species) — yet I
thank Him every day that He practiced that little deception
because if He hadn't, I wouldn't be sitting here writing about
my religious vocation.

THE POWER OF THE HAIL MARY

SISTER MARY LEONELLA, S.N.J.M.[1]

AS I swung on the gate that frosty November evening, waiting for Father to come home from his store, my mind was full of happy thoughts. When I threw back my head I could see the sky and the tips of the fir trees. When the gate was wide open I faced the house, big and comfortable against the dark background of evergreens. When the gate clicked shut I faced the mountains and the trees and the store. There was only one wagon left at the hitching post. Pretty soon Father would lock up and come home. When I grew up I would marry a nice man like Father and we would live right here on the Applegate River, with vineyards and orchards on the slope and mountains all around.

"This is the nicest place in the world," I crooned as I

---

[1] *Sister Mary Leonella was born at Kirbyville, Oregon, but when she was two years of age her parents moved to a ranch on the Applegate River, where she lived until she entered the novitiate of the Sisters of the Holy Names of Jesus and Mary. After sixty-six years as a very happy religious, many of them spent as a science professor at Marylhurst College in Oregon, Sister Leonella now devotes her time to praying, sewing, and directing the landscaping and gardening of the College property. The mother house of this teaching community is in Outremont, Montreal, Canada, and the headquarters of the Oregon Province, to which Sister Leonella belongs, are at Marylhurst, near Portland, Oregon.*

swung back and forth. "This is the nicest place in the world and I'll never live anywhere else."

If I had known then what I know now, I would have answered, "Guess again, little Emma. You're going to a far, far better home, and something will happen tonight to set you on your way."

I slipped my hand into Father's and skipped up the path beside him. It took three hops for each long step of his, and I was so busy counting I didn't even look at the house.

Suddenly Father dropped my hand and said sharply, "Run around to the front door. I'll see what's wrong here."

I knew he didn't want me to, but I looked toward the kitchen porch. There was a man lying on the steps.

In a few minutes Father came in.

"There's a poor fellow out there asking for food," he said. "He is so nearly starved that he fainted."

"Let me take him some dinner," I cried.

Ah Sing, the Chinese cook, served me a bowl of steaming soup and a heaped-up plate of meat and vegetables. As I gave them to the man he smiled at me, but his hands trembled. When he had taken the soup he leaned back, coughing.

"I can't eat any more," he said. "You are kind, ma petite. The good God will bless you. Now I must move on."

"Then I'll get you some shoes," I promised, and back into the house I ran.

"May I have some of your shoes for the poor stranger?" I asked Father. "All he has on his feet is gunny-sacking."

"To be sure," said Father.

But when I brought the shoes, the poor man had hardly strength to put them on. He was very tired and very sick. There would be no use in asking to keep him overnight in our house, for Father was particular about strangers.

"Can't he sleep in my playhouse?" I begged.

"That's a good idea, John," said Mother. "You put up a bed there and I'll get sheets and blankets."

Mother nursed our guest through a siege of pneumonia, and before he was fully well he had become a permanent member of the household. Henri LeChenault was a good man, refined and a skilled worker. Each year he tended the vineyard from spring to fall, and in the winter he mined the cinnabar needed to provide mercury for Father's gold mine.

And he taught me the Hail Mary.

That was a beautiful prayer, with phrases that rolled musically on my tongue and strange words that had a holy sound. Henri told me to say it every day and I never, never forgot. "Hail Mary . . . Holy Mary . . . pray for us now . . ."

The teachers who came and went never taught us about Holy Mary, Mother of God. They were able young teachers, for the most part, engaged to live at our house and tutor us. Miss Grore was the only one who talked about the Catholic religion; and she mentioned it in hushed tones to me when the others were not around. She talked of the horrors of convent life as described in *The Awful Disclosures of Maria Monk*. There were clanking chains in her stories, and walled-in nuns; there were dungeons and tunnels and nefarious schemes. I listened in guilty fascination. Mother would not want me to hear these wicked things, and she probably wouldn't believe them. She loved Catholics, like her dear friend Mrs. Orth in Jacksonville. But the stories must be true for Miss Grore had seen them in a printed book with pictures of nuns on the cover.

When Miss Grore's term ended, the stories ended, too. Once in a while after that, when I was alone in the dark, I would see a face behind iron bars or hear shrieks from a dungeon, but gradually the horrors faded from my mind as it was filled with better things. George Hoffman was teaching us now. He was a scholarly young German employed to keep books for Father and delighted at a chance to share his learning. So we studied algebra and geometry, botany, literature, ancient history — but not the meaning of the Hail Mary.

When I was fourteen I went to boarding school. My sister
Ellen had already finished her course at St. Mary's Academy
in Jacksonville, and I was to take her place. At first thought
I felt a faint, uneasy stirring — *The Awful Disclosures*. Pshaw,
that was nonsense. Ellen loved the nuns and our parents said
they were ladies and scholars.

"There would be very little culture in Southern Oregon if
it weren't for the Sisters of the Holy Names," Mother used
to say.

So we stitched and packed to get my outfit ready, and on
a sunny day we drove in the buggy down the river road to
Jacksonville. After tea with Mrs. Orth and her school-girl
daughter Jo, we went to the Academy where the sisters gave
us a friendly welcome. It was a good idea, they agreed, that
I had come early to get acquainted with the school before the
other pupils arrived. I was not so sure. When Mother left at
dusk, misgivings overcame me. There *was* a high hedge around
the convent yard, and a sister *did* slide the bolt on the hall
door. She was a round-faced, smiling sister, but maybe that
smile was a mask and those black robes cloaked a deceitful
heart. I had my supper alone in a high-ceilinged room designed
for fifty girls, and at bedtime I lay in a shuttered dormitory
of empty white cots. Try as I might, I could not evade *The
Awful Disclosures*. These nuns had hoodwinked Ellen. That
was a creaking of chains now — no, it was the wind in the
shutters. But those really were whirring groans that died away
when the hall clock struck the quarter hour, only to recur
in a few minutes. If this hideous night ever ended, I would
go to Mrs. Orth's and never come back.

But I did come back. Mrs. Orth faced my problem squarely.

"Homesickness has set your nerves on edge," she said. "That
Maria was neither a nun nor a Catholic, and she was never
within a hundred miles of the Hotel Dieu she pretended to
describe. Let's not mention her in the same breath with our
sisters, angels of mercy that they are. Anyone in Jacksonville

will tell you how they saved this town in the smallpox epidemic, by volunteering as nurses when everyone else was in a panic. The Sisters of the Holy Names aren't a nursing order, either, but teachers."

Good teachers they were. They assigned me to the second academic class, where I sat next to Jo Orth for every period but one: when she had Christian Doctrine I had to go with the other non-Catholics to study in the boarding-school room. I always went regretfully. If I didn't study Christian Doctrine, how could I ever fathom the meaning of the Hail Mary? I knew a little about it by now. Ellen had told me it was a part of the rosary, and I learned some of the mysteries from looking at pictures on the walls. When I asked Sister Sebastian for a rosary, though, she thought I was teasing. She finally saw that I was in earnest and not only gave me the beads but showed me how to use them.

On St. Patrick's Day of the next year I had my first chance to attend catechism. The boarding-school stove was out of order, so we were allowed to stay in the warm classroom. Sister Mary Flavia spent the period recounting the missionary activities of St. Patrick. As I listened, the thought occurred to me, "If St. Patrick could make Catholics out of the whole Irish nation, why can't he make a Catholic out of me?" It was the first time I had definitely realized my desire for baptism.

All I needed to do, it seemed, was to pray to St. Patrick. But how can you pray to a saint when his picture is in the reception room? It would look silly to kneel down in the midst of the fun, and you could never be alone in that room from morning till night.

Saturday evening as we reached the top of the dormitory stairs I asked permission to go back down. "No," said Sister Mary Florence.

"But I left my Sunday shoes in the recreation room. Really I did, Sister. I'm not going to play any tricks. Please, Sister."

Long afterward Sister told me that she had gone to the bend

of the staircase to look down upon whatever mischief might be under way. All she saw me do was to drop to my knees before the picture of the benign old Bishop. She didn't hear what I said, and as I came demurely into the dormitory, shoes in hand, I gave her no hint.

With St. Patrick's help, it was an easy matter to get my parents' consent for enrolling in the religion class. The next step was to begin instructions preparatory to my reception into the Church. I was baptized in my senior year, on the feast of Our Lady of Lourdes.

At my First Communion Mass next morning, Henri LeChenault knelt near me at the altar rail. He had come all the way from the cinnabar mine and was so happy he could only stroke my hair and say in a broken voice, "You were kind, ma petite. So I taught you the Hail Mary."

I couldn't say much, either. How could I tell Henri what the Hail Mary had meant to me? And how could I whisper even to myself the wonderful aspiration that was forming itself in my heart?

The girls at school talked a good deal about religious vocation. Jo Orth didn't want to be a sister. Helen McIntosh did. Ellen Caron was actually going to enter the novitiate after graduation. No one suspected my secret, but I felt happy inside.

Our home was in a joyous bustle that summer over the birth of my sister's son. For two years now, Ellen had been Mrs. George Hoffman — it was she who married a nice man like Father and made her home on the Applegate. My future seemed more complicated. I knew that some day I would be a nun, but how, and when? It was one thing for my parents to admire the sisters, and quite another thing to give them a daughter. The sisters themselves were not enthusiastic about taking me: I was a new convert, perhaps obsessed with a young girl's romantic dreams, and my application met a response that was sympathetic but scarcely encouraging. At least, it was not a flat refusal like Father's, and I thought it worth while to enlist St. Patrick's help.

"If you could make Catholics out of me and the whole Irish nation," I told him, "you can get me into the convent."

He took me there by a roundabout way that led me first to Jacksonville as an assistant teacher at the Academy. From the familiar surroundings I wrote again to Mother Provincial, and this time she answered, "Come."

"The opposition of your dear parents was to be expected," the letter went on. "However, you have much to be grateful for in the consent of your mother and the neutrality of your father toward the step you are about to take. Time, but above all the grace of God, which you are to implore for them early and late, will make unforeseen changes and the day may come when on bended knees they will bless the life you have chosen."

That prophecy never came true in Father's case, but it was literally fulfilled in Mother's. Every night she prayed for her children, each in turn, and when she came to my name she always said: "Thank God! one, at least, is safe."

I was a religious long professed when she died. All during her last day she had tried to convey some message, and my brothers and sisters told me, "There is something she wants you to do." Not until evening, when I happened to be alone with her, did I divine her thoughts.

"Mother, do you want me to baptize you?" A smile over-spread her face and she nodded eagerly. I poured water on her forehead and said the saving words, "Elizabeth, I baptize thee in the name of the Father and of the Son and of the Holy Ghost."

But that was long after the summer day when I went direct from the Academy to the novitiate in Portland, without going home. That seemed the better way. I never saw my father again; but please God, he is waiting for me in heaven.

In the novitiate Ellen Caron, a white-veiled novice, was the "Guardian Angel" appointed to help me get accustomed to unfamiliar ways. The gentle Mistress of Novices was my former boarding-school prefect, and Helen McIntosh was a fellow postulant.

There was no lack of Christian Doctrine lessons here. The beginning class was in "methods of Prayer," and the very first assignment was to memorize a passage that went something like this: "In meditating on the *Ave*, take the phrase 'Hail Mary' and endeavor to relish its sweetness as long as it will excite your devotion. Draw comparisons that may help you to enter into its meaning. Do the same with each word or group of words, uttering them gradually, one after the other. . . . At the following exercise, begin by saying the same prayer as far as the word which has already engaged your attention and touched your heart. . . ."

Last July I completed sixty-six years of religious life. Today I am telling the story of how I became a nun. This happens to be the twenty-fifth of March, the feast of the first Hail Mary.

FULFILLMENT

SISTER M. GRETCHEN, S.S.J.[1]

EVERYONE wants to get the most out of
life. Naturally. How foolish not to. We
have only one life. Every rational creature wants it to be a full
one. That is a universal premise. It would seem, therefore,
that I should begin with an apology for my life. I certainly
chose a strange way of getting the most out of life. When I
stop to think of it, don't I have to say to myself: "You are in
an unusual way of life, and you haven't an excuse in the world
for being there"? If I do, then I have to answer: "Am I? It
doesn't seem unusual to me . . . and . . . I never looked for an
excuse." That's so. People don't have excuses for getting married, except that they fall in love. And of course there's no
excuse for falling in love. Vocation is another word for love.
There's no excuse for it, and there's no defense for it . . .
except love.

There is no one moment, no one circumstance. The seed of
a vocation falls into a soul — how or when is not always certain;
but it grows there and makes itself evident by many a little
sign along the way. These signs are different for each person.
I've asked many sisters how they knew they had a vocation,

---

[1] *Sister M. Gretchen, of Brighton, Massachusetts, belongs to the
Congregation of the Sisters of St. Joseph of Boston, a teaching community. Sister Gretchen is Director of Speech and Drama at Mount
St. Joseph Academy, 637 Cambridge Street, Brighton 35, Massachusetts. This is also the address of the mother house.*

hoping some pattern might emerge, but I can only report that God has called us to religion in as many ways as there are sisters. If anyone doubts that His finger is in our lives, that nothing is accidental, let him ask any group of nuns how each happened to come to the convent. For myself, when I was in the sixth grade and the class was assigned a composition on "My Vocation," I wrote: "I would like to be a sister, but I do not want to be a common ordinary sister." (I probably had the Carmelite Order in mind for myself.) I remember this clearly because my very understanding sixth grade teacher asked me, with a twinkle in her eye, whether she were the "common ordinary" kind I had referred to. I admitted that she was. Years later I wrote to that sister: "I have decided to become a 'common ordinary' sister, if they will have a 'common ordinary' girl."

So much had happened between that first remark and the second, but it had all happened inside me. How to tell what cannot really be told at all. As someone has said, "My secret is my own." But I will try to share it.

During my high school days I threw myself wholeheartedly into the business of being young. I loved doing everything there was to do in school and out of it. How precious was life, "the mere living," as Browning puts it. I liked people and being with them, but I was always aware that beneath the fun we had, beneath our long talks about everything under the sun, there were things I did not and could not share, things that mattered, things that I couldn't put into words even for myself. They weren't my dreams for the future. These dreams were ambitious but all quite easy to name: dreams of being a dress designer, a character actress, a newspaper reporter, the creator of a new comic strip, a writer, a senator — those glowing dreams you have in your teens when everything is possible. About these things I could talk easily with my friends, and laugh, too, because I took them only half seriously.

Something else was growing in me, some other need for fulfillment far beyond these dreams. I knew it only when I

made visits to church and knelt before the tabernacle. Then I
was understood; then I began to understand that nothing mattered except finding out what it was that God wanted of me. In
other moments, too, I was aware of God: walking up a hill,
looking up at the stars, facing into the wind. I used to love to
swim way out with my back to the shore so that I could see only
sky and sea . . . swim slowly . . . to exult in the glory of the
earth. In all these moments I desired to be made one with and
to serve forever the Creator of heaven and earth and all things.
But how this was to be done I did not ask. So far these feelings
were not urgent; they were shaping up for some far future; I
was busy being seventeen.

Then one day at the beginning of my senior year in high
school, an inspiring teacher it was my good fortune to have at
this crucial hour said to me, "Did you ever think of being a
sister?" That was all she said, but it was enough. The question
had been put and I had to answer it. I wasn't sure I wanted to
give the answer just then, but the answer was already in
my heart.

"In a nutshell," as my grandmother would say, the matter
stood thus: God had been good to me. I loved Him. I wanted to
give Him a gift. Now someone had suggested the possibility of
giving all my life. From that moment, anything short of everything would have been shabby. It only remained for me to
say, "Yes."

A vocation is the "pearl of great price," "costing not less than
everything," as T. S. Eliot says. But that is exactly why boys
and girls still want it, still stand ready to pay the price. The
young are glorious in giving. I made my decision. The only one
who tried to shake it was a family friend, a successful and per-
suasive gentleman. He told me I hadn't really had time to
know what I was leaving. I couldn't answer his arguments with
any "knockdown" ones of my own. I could now. But then I
was inarticulate with youth and love, inarticulate but very sure
in heart. So I took that giant step away from home and familiar

ways, the step that is harder for those who let you go than it is for you, ardent and impetuous as you are at the time. Almost, the great "Let it be done" is theirs to say on that day. It is to those dear ones, after God, that I owe first gratitude for my vocation.

I turned my face to the "September hill," the hill I love in Framingham. The very air up there is like new wine, and visibility is one hundred per cent for the great pattern, the wide horizons, the true meaning of life. But the schedule was very simple, very normal. Nothing was asked of us except to obey the rules and to learn a new point of view, the eternal point of view. I had braced myself for rigors that never came (save the daily rigor of rising to the five-thirty clang: an indignity that did not grow easier with the years, as our Mistress of Novices warned us). Before I entered I had been a little afraid that I would not be able to be myself, to say what I thought and felt any more. This went hard with me, but I had to enter anyway. After entering I was relieved to find that I could raise my hand and give my own answers to questions that were asked in our classes; to find that I could be natural even while trying to be supernatural; to learn that God always builds on what we bring to Him, which is what He gave us in the first place.

And no one can deny that it was good to be there with seventy-five other girls: no two alike but all of us *keen* for this new life, all of us *green* to it — earnest, trying, making mistakes, laughing, going on, experiencing a wonderful *esprit de corps*, together in study, recreation, conferences, prayer.

We were only six months away from ankle socks on March 19, the day we received the habit. A very long line of radiant brides approached the altar rail that afternoon. I remember happiness and excitement. I remember, too, that they served raspberry sauce for supper. This seemed a stroke of mismanagement to me, who had all I could do to bring the spoon up over the new expanse of white under my chin, without adding the threat of raspberry sauce. My habit is now as much a part of me as hand

or arm, but my awkwardness in it then was quite typical of my
newness to the life. Much as I looked the part that day, I was
yet a great way off from being a real sister.

Three years later I went to the altar to pronounce my vows,
bearing a lighted candle as symbol of the life I wished to burn
out in God's service. The day I received my Profession Cross,
the Cross of Christ as visible pledge of God's acceptance, that
was the day I became a Sister of St. Joseph, the happiest day of
my life. On that day no sister feels that she is giving up anything. She is overwhelmed with a sense of her own beggary, of
the great love God has shown her. For myself, there was, deep
within my soul, a singing certainty that I was where I was meant
to be, where God wanted me to be, and that was all that mattered. I was one with the will behind the harmony of the universe, the will which alone could make sense out of human life.

There are many things in religious life that are incommuni-
cable, but one tangible joy I may mention and eagerly take this
opportunity of doing so. It is the joy of incorporation with a
group of splendid human beings — my sisters in religion. Perfect? No. It is a mark of immaturity to demand perfection of
anyone except oneself. Someone has said that not even the
saints are safely saints until fifteen minutes after they're dead.
You and I know that though you should clothe a girl in twenty
religious habits, she would still be the same girl underneath
(slightly smothered) that all her life had made of her. No,
sisters are human beings. Their only glory and their only perfection is in their dedication. But perhaps nowhere else in the
world does there exist a group of people so varied and yet so
single-minded; a group who have put every other thing in life
aside and paid all they had for what they held most high. Among
them women gifted as administrators, homemakers, teachers,
artists, conversationalists, musicians . . . but all of them women
who have set aside the good things of this world, not because
they loved them less but because they loved something else more
— God's will.

Christ said, "Wherever two or more are gathered together in My name, there am I in the midst of them." That is exactly what I have felt many times — at recreation, in chapel, at meals, anywhere. There is a support and joy here, a solidarity of purpose and of charity that bears you along. It is part of the hundredfold: refreshment, strength, encouragement, challenge — all these my sisters give to me just by living their lives around me. Things they never say that I can see, these gladden the heart even in a human way, these I offer to God when my own offering falls so far short. When you have belonged to such a group, borne the burdens of the heat and of the day, shared the same faith, the same vision, you are bound by more than ordinary ties and you owe a more than ordinary allegiance. One sentence in our office gains in significance through the years: "I have taken root in an honorable people."

But isn't this life monotonous? The instantaneous response to that question from sisters everywhere is a smile. Religious life is everything else before it is monotonous. A convent is one of the busy places of the world. I remember, though, that I also wondered what sisters did with their time. But since the day I entered I haven't had a chance to wonder, for I haven't had one spare moment. All of us found that every thought, every talent we'd ever had, everything we'd ever learned to do, even if it were only to play the piano with one finger, was called into service; we found ourselves playing the piano with one finger while we used the other nine for something else.

Have I found happiness? I put that question to another sister. Without the slightest hesitation, as though she had been ready with her answer for years just waiting for someone to ask, she said, "Sister, every new day brings its new joys." That's the answer. For those who have followed a religious vocation, there's nothing like it.

But isn't it hard? The religious life is not easy. But happiness was never a matter of ease. Youth does not ask that life be easy — only that it be great. And greatness, what is that? There

is only one way to personal greatness. Only one. The giants of
this earth are those who, by God's grace, are equal to the will
of God. Today we have so many frustrated people because there
are so few who can take the going-wrong of their own plans and
desire the going-right of God's plans. They are out of joint
with themselves because they are out of joint with God. There
are no greater people than those who lift up their lives in a
toast to the wonderful will of God. This is success. The only
success that is immortal. And so I come to the simple fact, a
fact you know: that there is no comparison between one way
of life and another. In God's will we find fulfillment. His will
is the vocation of every one of us. And if he calls you to religious
life, you will never be completely out of it. No social work, no
lay apostolate will ever take the place, for you, of giving yourself in the total surrender that the religious life asks.

But how does such a life of renunciation satisfy the human
need for love? How can anyone talk about a full life and not
mention love? How can life be full without love? It cannot, of
course. And yet, so many people do not know what love is.
Most young people seek a full life in marriage. For many that
little phrase, "until death," is too much, asks too much. They
bind themselves for as long as the feeling lasts; they bind
themselves "for better" but not "for worse." And so for them
love never begins at all. In every walk of life the name of love-
come-true is fidelity. I linger upon that word, that beautiful
word: *fidelity*. The modern world has no use for it. That is why
the modern world is frustrated — because fidelity is the secret of
fulfillment. It is the last farthing you pay for something you
want more than anything else. For those who really love, "until
death" is not enough. They desire love that is "stronger than
death." Every young girl desires that such love and such fidelity
illumine her life.

In my work as Director of Dramatics I have written and
produced several full-length plays. In all of these plays there
are, of course, love scenes. Some people have expressed surprise

that a nun could write an authentic love scene, but these people do not know or have not stopped to think that a nun is a full-fledged human being. She knows, or should know, better than anyone else what love is and the beauty of it. She came to God bringing in her two hands all the love she had ever known, all the love it was possible for her ever to know, and she brought that as a gift good and precious, saying, "Take and receive, O Lord, all my love — with all my life." God thought of love before the human heart thought of it. God *is* love. And when you begin to love God, then you begin to know what love is.

Every human heart echoes with the great "Quo vadis?" Where are you going? What is the point of it all? Where is it, that which you seek? For me it is in the religious life. I have found that which I sought, and now there remains fidelity to it. Every night I go down on my knees and thank God for my vocation. I know I am not and never will be worthy of it. But I love it. I ask only to serve Him as a bungling and "unprofitable" servant, as a "common ordinary" Sister of St. Joseph, all the days of my life. I know that "one day in His courts is better than thousands" out of them. To consummate that vocation, to bring it "until death" — to me that is the great miracle, the perfect fulfillment. Only God can work miracles. This I ask of Him.

In my present position I have seen the morning star rise in other eyes — in the eyes of some of our finest girls. Every September they turn their faces toward the hill in Framingham, faces beautiful with promise, eyes shining with dedication. And I bow my head and I know the meaning of the word *vocation.*

"AND THE WALLS
CAME TUMBLING DOWN..."

SISTER MARY BASIL, S.S.N.D.[1]

WHEN I was nine years old my sister left home to become a nun. She was wearing a brown suit with bright red buttons, and her dark hair and dark eyes shone under the gay little hat that was almost new. I thought she was very lovely and wondered if the sisters would think so too. The teachers in our parish school were good, practical women, but I did not think they had ever worn a brown suit with red buttons, and my imagination refused to consider the question of hair.

I knew they were human beings. I could even smile myself when Mother entertained company with the story of my solemn announcement (after three weeks in first grade) that I was going to be a sister because all a sister had to wash was her face and hands. I knew now they were human beings, quite ordinary human beings, who washed and swept and taught school, and loved God a great deal. But I knew too I was not going to be one! I was not going to be one!

Sis came home for a visit before her reception as a School

---

[1] *Sister Mary Basil was born in Escanaba, Michigan. Trained as a teacher and an accountant, she worked in both professions before entering the convent. Now a School Sister of Notre Dame, Sister Mary Basil is Assistant Commissary General at the mother house of her community, Notre Dame Convent, 1324 North Milwaukee Street, Milwaukee 1, Wisconsin.*

Sister of Notre Dame. She was different — not too much so, but different. The light in her eyes was still there, quieter, like candles glowing in a dark room. She laughed just as much, and teased me even more, but there was a wall between us, a shadowy wall, casting queer patterns, and built of days she had spent in the candidature doing things in which I had no part, learning things I did not know. Sometimes I caught her looking at me in a strange, analytical way, and when we went to church together I had a panicky feeling, kneeling next to her slim, upright figure, that she was praying for me.

"She's praying me into the convent," I thought, and my heart charged with a sickening lurch, as though I were going down, down in a fast elevator. With a determination born of desperation I resolved to out-pray her. My whole life was before me, wrapped up like a Christmas present. I could not see what was inside; time would unwrap the package, a little bit at a time. But there was going to be no long black dress in it for me, no long black veil, and certainly no rule book. I was going to live my own life as I wished.

I would be a good Catholic, of course, and I would serve God. But I could do that at home. My mother did. And so, my daily prayers were threaded with an ever recurring fiber of inconsistency: "Dear Lord, help me to do Your will, but please don't want me to be a nun. Please don't want me to be a nun."

The prayer served as insulation against the kindness of my teachers. High school was a protection against thought. The immediate present was my security, and I piled my classes, my books, my friends, our parties, our dancing, our brittle schoolgirl happiness as a barricade against the future.

During my senior year Sister Mary Bruno tried to get past the impasse.

"Have you ever thought of being a sister, Clara?" she asked casually one day.

The vehemence of my negative answer must have surprised her unless, as I suspect, her shrewd wisdom discovered my cul-de-sac. Perhaps she joined her prayers to my sister's — I do not know. Perhaps she reported my excited reaction to my other teachers, and they too began a siege of prayers. I do not know.

At any rate, they left me alone, and my last months in high school were undisturbed. At Marquette Normal I felt safe; there were no nuns and no vocational problems. I finished at Normal, and at seventeen I received my first assignment — teaching in an eight-grade country school in Burnt Bluff. Some day, perhaps, I shall write a book about that year, for there were enough stories to make one. Some of the boys in the eighth grade were as old as I, many were bigger. But we got along famously, and I loved the challenge of teaching. My transfer to Nahma Public School the next year, with only third, fourth, and fifth grades was decidedly less exciting. But there were more dances at Nahma, and I missed none of them.

The thin wraith of a religious vocation seemed to have blown away, but I still said my prayer to be spared, just in case. The "just in case" was bigger than I admitted, even to myself. I found myself restless, not quite satisfied with a very satisfactory teaching position, not quite satisfied with dances, not at all satisfied with myself.

"But what do you want?" my mother probed.

I did not quite know myself, but it would not do to admit it. I wanted something different, I wanted to get away. And then I remembered the mathematics professor who had commented on my work at Normal. "You would make a good accountant," he had said.

The memory gave me an idea. "I want to be a certified public accountant," I burst out, "and I want to travel."

Anthony Wayne Institute at Fort Wayne, Indiana, trained CPA's, and I went there, my mother consenting reluctantly to the many miles between us. A business career may be pure prose, but my dreams were absolute poetry. I would begin as an accountant, of course. I might even consent to be a secretary, and I took shorthand, typing, and business law to make sure that I held all the keys to an administrative position. I was going to be a businesswoman, not a stenographer, an accountant, not a bookkeeper. Divine Wisdom must have smiled at my plans, knowing how soon He was going to shatter them, and how later, when they meant nothing at all, give them back.

My work at Anthony Wayne finished, I came to Milwaukee armed with a letter of introduction to an auditor. Coincidence, which is often a synonym for the working of Divine Providence, began to roll its rocks into the path of my plans. They were all small rocks, pebbles, really, but they had to be removed. Mr. Bullock did God's work by not being on hand for the promised interview, and my sister, who always did God's work, continued to serve Him in St. Elizabeth's School in the same city.

I went to see her, and found myself back in the old role of little sister, wailing out a litany of unbelievable woe. I had not anticipated Mr. Bullock's being out of town. I had not looked for rooms because I was not sure I could get the position. I could not go home for fear he would return and give the position to someone else. I could not stay indefinitely in a Milwaukee hotel for I didn't have that kind of money.

"I'll ask Sister Eulogia if you can stay here with us until you know what you are going to do," my sister suggested.

Stay in a convent! My heart stopped short, and then jumped in quick, emphatic disapproval. But she did not hear my heart, and my lips, silenced by my need, made no objections.

I stayed at the convent in the guest room — a curiously high-ceilinged strip of space with sash windows, furnished simply and soberly with the mid-Victorian furniture of some parishioner who had moved and donated his old bedroom set to the sisters. I stayed at the convent even after I had my appointment, even after I got my first job as an accountant. No one suggested that I leave, and I found myself hoping that no one would. Even when gentle Sister Eulogia said she would pray for me I was not frightened.

"Pray that I get the kind of work I want," I said, and her eyes had been amused as she answered, "I will."

"Would you like to go to recreation with us?" my sister asked one evening.

"Doing what?" I answered, more than a little doubtful of the entertainment value of the tepid games that would be served up.

"We can play parchesi," my sister said simply.

"Parchesi!" I thought of the dance I had attended the night before, and wondered what the office crowd would think if they could see me carefully moving the little colored disks down a cardboard path.

"Oh, come on, Clara," Sis said unexpectedly. "Don't be so ultrasophisticated."

"I'm not being ultrasophisticated," I snapped, and then laughed. Parchesi was certainly no matter for controversy.

I went, and that night in bed, looking back on what had honestly been a pleasant evening, wondered at myself as much as at the nuns. I was changing; there was no question about it. I was not only changing; I had changed. The tide of desire that had pushed me to Milwaukee had receded, and a business career seemed to mean and matter less and less. I had come to love the consecrated women whose guest I was, whose family spirit was so vitalizing a force, whose kindness to one another and to me was so casual, so unobtrusive, and so real.

My sister knew what had happened before I did, and her prayers for me shifted from petition to thanksgiving long before the day I knelt in the little convent chapel to tell God, "It's all right about that religious vocation. I'll go." Then I wrote to Mother.

Her answer was immediate and uncompromising, "Come home." Poor Mother! She had been willing to let my sister enter the convent, but both her daughters! Surely even God did not expect that!

I went home to her pleading, to her little involved contrivances to have me meet the right boys, boys I had known in grade school, who were no more interested in me than I was in them. We played the game, Mother and I, an armed truce ruling for days. I took a position at the Escanaba National Bank, and tried to live the old life for her sake, to fill the days with the things that had been so satisfying such a short time before. But it was no use.

It was not that I had grown pietistic; it was not that I did not enjoy dancing, or parties or people. It was not that I did not love my family. I had tasted something at St. Elizabeth's Convent, and could not stop hungering for it. When spring came, I again brought up the subject of my leaving, but Mother was adamant.

"I won't give up both my daughters," she said firmly. "At least, I won't give them up willingly."

"What would you do if I just went?" I asked, and immediately I felt ashamed of myself, as I always did at the quick hurt in her eyes. This was the punishment, surely, for the years when I had begged God not to ask me to be particularly His. Now when I wanted more than anything in the world to give myself, I could not without hurting terribly the one person least deserving hurt of my making. I dared not ask God to change her mind now that I had changed mine. But what I did not dare He did.

A telegram from New York called Mother to my brother Theodore, who, the telegram said, was critically ill. What happened on that long, lonely trip to New York, in the slow hours while she watched him fight with death and win, I shall never know. I cannot say she gave me to God if his life would be spared. She never said.

She simply came home — white, spent, and smiling, and in her smile was her propitiation. We both knew the uselessness of words.

August was rapidly coming to a close, and I was torn between the desire to enter the convent immediately, on the regular entrance day, August 28, and my wish not to appear ungrateful to my kind employer by giving so short a notice of my intentions, without sufficient time to initiate my successor. Then, suddenly, the man whose position I had taken in the bank came back to town, and in his joblessness I found the answer to the gnawing question: When?

There was nothing to keep me now; Mother was willing, and I myself wanted nothing more than this. On the feast of St. Augustine I left home for the mother house of the School Sisters of Notre Dame, tearing down the last of the protective bulwark for self a little girl of nine had built against God.

I have done many things in the convent, and religious life has held many surprises. I have found unusual things in unexpected places, but the most amusingly ironic has been the complete fulfillment of my early plans now that fulfillment does not matter. As bursar of the community, accounting is my business, and I never step on a train or a plane without remembering my dreams of travel. And I never travel without luxuriating in the thought that at the end of the journey I will be home.

FROM ALL ETERNITY

SISTER MARY CORDA, P.B.V.M.[1]

WE WERE playing blocks together, my brother and I, when I said in a tone which I hoped would be stern enough to make an impression on his five-year-old mind, "You are not going to call me 'Margaret' any more."

"I'm not?" he said, raising startled brown eyes and holding two blocks poised in mid-air. "What am I going to call you?"

"You are going to call me 'sister,'" I announced solemnly. Skepticism was written deep on my brother's face, but being a child of few words, all he said was, "Why?"

I explained patiently. "Because I want everybody to call me that. But I have to start with someone so I am starting with you. If you call me 'sister' then all the other children in the neighborhood will too, and after a while," I ended on a nice triumphant note, "everyone in the whole world will call me 'sister.'"

This childish plan was not, I am afraid, very successful with my brother, but years later, after I had entered the Catholic Church and received the holy habit of religion, I remembered that plan of a child who had never heard of such a person as a

---

[1] *Sister Mary Corda was born into a Protestant family in Pomona, California. She lost her faith while she was in college, but later regained more than she had lost, for shortly after her graduate studies in psychology at a large secular university she entered the Catholic Church. A year later she became a Sister of the Presentation of the Blessed Virgin Mary at Aberdeen, South Dakota.*

Catholic nun and yet who wanted somehow to be to everyone all the things that the term "sister" implies. Yet even this desire which the good God had already planned to grant in a more wonderful way than a Protestant child could possibly imagine was not the beginning of my vocation. To me it seems that in conscious awareness it had its dim beginnings when I was only three years old. True, I was twenty-five when I found the Catholic Church and chose to enter the convent; however this was not the beginning, rather the end of a long, long road. We humans choose God in time, but Infinite Love chooses us who are to be His spouses from all eternity.

So tiny, so seemingly insignificant, those early memories of mine — walking round and round in a dizzy circle with the tiny child's delight in pure movement, chanting at the same time the Apostles' Creed — "I believe in God, the Father Almighty, Maker of Heaven and Earth. . . . I believe in the Holy Catholic Church" — words difficult for me to pronounce clearly, impossible to comprehend. Twenty-two years were to pass before I would kneel and with complete understanding, profess again my faith in the Catholic Church. There are other memories too: the sight of a monk framed in an archway of the old mission at San Juan Capistrano, the majestic thunder of voices in the Hallelujah Chorus, "And He shall reign for ever and ever."

There are later memories, too, painful, haunting ones; questions asked and not answered because those I asked knew no answers; the darkness of confusion when the developing intellect begins to wonder what is true and one hears on all sides, "Nobody knows." Sometimes, it seems, one must lose all one has in order to possess at last much more. Sometimes we must even feel that we have lost God Himself. It was this way with me as one doctrine after another seemed to be slipping away. Words spoken by men in good faith can be terrible things. "Christ was only speaking figuratively. Bread and wine do not become His Body and His Blood." "No angels sang when He was born." "He was a great man but He was not God." God permits us to remember such words all our lives, not that we may suffer again as we did when we first heard them, but in order that we may pray for those who spoke them and who still walk in the darkness.

Strangely enough, I lost my faith in a Protestant religious college, and I regained it in the graduate school of a great secular university where everything seemed to be against ever believing in anything. Yet it was in this atmosphere of complete skepticism that I came to believe again in God, the Father Almighty, and in the divinity of His Son. Perhaps this seems like very little to be sure of, but it marked for me the beginning of the dawn.

When I entered graduate school, I felt that I had very little faith, but in comparison with most of my companions I had a great deal. In the long discussions which we frequently had, I usually found myself alone in arguing that man was not just an animal, that absolute truth did exist, that morality was not purely subjective and, above all, that there was a God. My friends regarded these "antiquated notions" with considerable tolerance, confident, no doubt, that I would soon come around to their way of thinking. It puzzled me greatly that so many people seemed not to want to believe in a personal God — that they did not feel they needed Him. I wanted to believe and I wanted more than anything else to find the Father and His Son again. And then, suddenly, when everything seemed very dark, all was changed. Just as a child knows that the sun is warm because he feels its heat, so I knew that there was a personal God because I felt His love.

In my first months in the Catholic Church, I was frequently asked one question in tones varying from mild curiosity to something very like anger and resentment — asked by priests, Catholic lay people, Protestants, and pagans. "Why did you enter the Catholic Church?" I was almost afraid to tell them the truth. It was so unlike what they were expecting. It would have been much easier if I could have said something like this: "After long study of its doctrines, I am convinced that it is the true Church," or perhaps, "I plan to marry a Catholic," or even "I feel attracted by the beauty of the Church with its music and art." However, none of these things was true. The only reason I stood one May afternoon at the door of a Catholic rectory to ask for instruction was that I believed with all my heart that Jesus Christ was present in the tabernacle of every Catholic Church. Since only Catholics believed this, there was only one thing to do: I must belong to their Church.

During the days of instruction and reading in the great new field of literature that had suddenly opened to me, I learned the other things that Catholics believed and I believed them too. I learned proofs and reasons which appealed to my intellect, and I realized how good it was thus to put one's faith on the foundation of knowledge, but without that first gift of faith which comes from God alone, no knowledge and no arguments are of any use. Sometimes one hears new converts complain about their bewilderment and loneliness during their first few months in the Church. For me there was only the joy of coming home, the joy of reunion with the God I had loved so much and thought I had lost forever.

When I became a Catholic I had learned, by one method or another, a great deal about the Church, but I knew almost nothing about the religious life. I felt very shy on the few occasions I had to speak with nuns, and life in the convent, as I imagined it, had absolutely no attraction. I liked my work as a child psychologist, and, with God, the world seemed a very wonderful place. A few days before my baptism I assured my mother, "I have to become a Catholic because I believe it is the true faith, but you don't need to worry ever about my going off to become a nun. A convent is no place for me." Mother agreed and said she was glad I felt that way, but somehow she did not sound quite convinced that I could be trusted on this matter, and, as it turned out, she was entirely right.

My firm resolve to have nothing to do with convents lasted until the day of my First Communion and then disappeared completely and permanently. The evening of that most beautiful day of my life I went around to the rectory to thank the young priest who had instructed me and to pick up a few more bits of information. I had a secret too, which I really meant to conceal, but much to my surprise, it burst out.

"Father," I said, "I know that I shall become a nun." Father controlled his facial expression admirably in view of the fact that it had been about twenty-four hours before that he had been pouring the waters of baptism over my head. No doubt he thought many things about the unreliable enthusiasm of new converts, but he said nothing and neither did I, having already said more than I wished. After all, there was nothing that could be said in words. That morning God had given Himself entirely to me, and I knew that in return I must belong entirely to Him. Instinctively I knew that the surest way to give myself completely to God was to enter the convent, although since the idea did not greatly appeal to me, I had every intention of postponing the step as long as possible.

Perhaps for the recent convert there is always a new brightness and wonder in life. Certainly it was that way for me. The world had never seemed so lovely. As St. John of the Cross expressed it long ago, "God Himself was mine and all for me because Christ was mine and all for me. . . . Mine were the angels and the Mother of God." In all my joy I saw clearly that the Cause of it all was hidden in the tabernacle, and I was drawn there at every possible opportunity. When my mother, to whom I had always been very close, followed me into the Church, my happiness seemed complete, but lurking in the back of my mind was the thought that I must one day leave her, the children I was trying to help, and a hundred less important things. I tried to reassure myself. "After all," I thought, "there is nothing I can do yet. No community in its right mind would even consider one who has been in the Church only a few months. I will have to wait at least two years, so I might as well enjoy myself in the meantime."

At this time my vocation was certainly not very strong. I longed for closer union with God, and I felt that the way to that union was marked by the cross, but as yet I had no desire to sacrifice anything. I wanted to be a successful psychologist, get a Ph.D. in a year or so, wear pretty clothes, and, above all, do my own will in all things. True, I wanted to enter the convent when it was possible to do so, but chiefly because I wanted to be close to God. To live under the same roof with our Lord in the Blessed Sacrament seemed to me, as it still does, the greatest joy that a human being could know on earth. I wanted that gift from God, too, but I did not understand that there is a price to be paid. I had not yet learned the great joy of giving something to God in return for all that He had given me.

Gradually during the next few months God put into my heart a desire without which perseverance in the religious life would be difficult, if not absolutely impossible: the desire to sacrifice and even to suffer for His sake. Before, all I had wished was to be with our Lord; now I wished to be in some small way like Him even in His suffering. The thought of what my friends, already puzzled at my entrance into the Catholic Church, would say when I entered a convent had troubled me a little; now I was quite willing that they should think me a fool. I had shrunk from leaving my mother alone; now, because He had left His Blessed Mother, I would leave mine too. I had loved my own way; now I wanted only His. I wanted the certainty of knowing God's will in little matters as well as great, and already I saw dimly that that knowledge would be one of the greatest joys of religious life. For me, still ignorant of these joys, the great attraction in the convent lay in the fact that I expected it to provide the opportunities for sacrifice which my soul was beginning to demand.

Now I felt an urgency that would not leave me. There seemed to be so little time. I wanted to leave the world quickly. Two years seemed far too long to wait. Surely, I thought, if it is God's will for me to enter a convent immediately, there must be somewhere in the world a community that will accept me. In my mind there was only one condition; it must be in another state where I knew no one. I hoped it might be one which engaged in the kind of work I had been trained to do, but even that no longer seemed very important.

My method of learning the will of God in this matter seemed quite simple and perfectly infallible. First I looked through Catholic magazines for the names and addresses of communities interested in receiving postulants. Then I began to write letters. I was sure that all of them would refuse so recent a convert, that is, all but one. The only reason I expected that even one would accept me was that I was certain that God wanted me to enter somewhere very soon. However, it soon proved that this ingenious plan was far from perfect. All of the superiors answered promptly and most kindly and, as I expected, most of them tactfully suggested that I restrain my enthusiasm and wait for a few years to "test" my vocation. Still, much to my amazement, several superiors at least held out some hope of my entrance soon. Now what was I to do? God let me puzzle over this problem for several months before He showed me the solution. In fact, He let me wait so long that I had decided to choose more or less at random one of those communities that had so kindly agreed to let me enter, but I was not quite happy about my decision.

When God calls souls to the religious life, it does not seem to me that His call is a kind of general summons to any of a thousand communities, but rather, like a loving Father, He chooses that place which is to be our new home, that particular spot where He sees we will give Him the greatest glory and sanctify our souls. He chooses for each of us a new mother who will teach us to walk in these strange new paths. He chooses our confessor and our sisters; all things are ordered by Him for our happiness. Because I believed all this, it does not seem strange to me that God should have inspired the sudden change in my plans and drawn me to a community which I had not even considered, but which He had chosen for me from all eternity.

It was in the month of our Lady that it happened, just as it had been in that month a year before that God had shown me His Church. Mother and I were saying the rosary together as we did so often, when the conviction was born in my mind that I was not to continue with my plans to enter the distant community I had chosen. Instead I was to go back to the town where I had been instructed in the Faith, to the Sisters of the Presentation of the Blessed Virgin Mary. In my excitement I interrupted my mother in the middle of a Hail Mary to say, "We must go to Aberdeen right away to see the sisters there, because if they will take me, that is where I am going."

During the whole of her religious life surely every sister, whatever may be her community, must praise and adore God for bringing her to the particular place where He wishes her to serve Him. As for me, from the first moment in the convent parlor as I waited to speak to the sister who was to be my new mother, I felt at home. Not that I wasn't a little bewildered and afraid, but underneath there was a kind of peace. I had wanted to help children and I learned that Nano Nagle, the holy foundress of the Presentation Sisters, had given her life for that very purpose. I had wanted to be near our Lord in the Blessed Sacrament; I discovered that here in the mother house the sisters enjoyed the great privilege of daily exposition of the Blessed Sacrament.

It was on our Lady's birthday, just as I had completed my first year in the Church, that I knelt to receive the postulant's cap. It is a simple ceremony, but one so beautiful that the memory of it does not fade even after the greater days of Reception of the Holy Habit and Profession. Feeling strange and awkward in my new black clothes, lonely in spite of the sisters' friendliness, I knelt with the other postulants in the

novitiate before the statue of our Blessed Mother. Suddenly
I was afraid, terribly afraid. Did God really want me? Had I
not been most presumptuous? What right had I to be here?
Then as I felt the cap being placed on my head, I saw God's
reassuring answer in the words printed in a little frame on
the wall before me, "You have not chosen Me, but I have
chosen you." These words entered deep into my heart that
afternoon. They were my strength in the days of the postulancy
and the novitiate, and they will be my joy forever. Wonder
of wonders, mystery never to be understood, and love un-
fathomable — to be chosen by God from all eternity — to belong
to Him alone forever!

CURTAIN CALL

SISTER M. LAURIAN, F.S.P.A.[1]

THE heavy maroon curtains slipped together with a velvet thud. Eager eyes sent congratulations to classmates for the wonderful job they had done on their parts, and the entire cast slipped silently back to the dressing rooms. Behind a fast disappearing coat of grease paint my gray matter was being tickled by the challenging thought, "Is there really anything that's more fun than drama?" Mental pictures of bicycling, boating, swimming, and riding synchronized themselves into a whirling holiday scene which teetered with acting on a hairline balance. But one doesn't roam or act one's whole life away really. And yet . . . what was it that Sister had said in the very first drama class way back in September? "If you don't want to be a fool for Christ's sake, you had better leave now and go to the office and sign up for another class." Naturally no one had gone and so there had been these nine wonderful months past in which the seniors didn't have to try too hard to be fools but did really try to be them for Christ's sake.

---

[1] *Sister Laurian of Ashland, Wisconsin, became deeply interested in dramatics during her high school days and seemed destined for a career in the theater. But God had a different idea and He inspired her to make a sudden decision in favor of the convent. Now, as a Sister of the Third Order of St. Francis of Perpetual Adoration, she teaches in Spokane, Washington. The mother house of this community is St. Rose Convent, La Crosse, Wisconsin.*

At first I thought it strange that there should be two patrons for the class. I could understand why St. Genesius was invoked because every Catholic who sets foot on the boards knows that this Roman is the patron of actors. But I was a little dubious about calling on St. Francis — much as I loved the Little Poor Man. Did he really fit in a drama class? Tonight had demonstrated that answer. Tonight the DePadua Thespians had paid their whole-souled tribute to the Little Man who had cast everything aside and had taken to the road to present to the public the tremendous drama of God's love for man. Depicting the life story of St. Francis had been the culmination of a year's study of God's troubadour, a year of loving imitation.

But once the class play is over seniors get a nagging feeling somewhere between the pit of their stomach and the depth of their heart. The reason for this ache is an attempt to find a place for themselves in the rocking boat of the world. Still another reason is the frontier of the future. Every time I tried to look into this great borderland which was said to be filled with so many dangers and opportunities, I found that my foresight was very myopic. Each squint would end up with the desperate pleading, "My God, what do You want me to do?" Soon that prayer was like a theme song running through my being. Its haunting melody would push itself through my consciousness at the most unexpected times: in the middle of a chemistry exam, while relaxing at a Sodality dance, after picking up a beautiful agate on the windy beaches of Lake Superior, or perhaps, during the breath-splitting two seconds between stanzas of a modern song. But a question such as this is often difficult to decide — not only because of ramifications and possibilities, but also because it is so easy to deceive oneself. When I was just a tiny child, I wanted to be a nun. I didn't quite know what it meant but I did know that the Little Flower was one and I loved her — but I loved my mother, too. Occasionally the thought would come that perhaps God did want me to be a nun and yet I didn't know.

Thus graduation found me with a diploma from high school and a scholarship for college in my hand but no definite resolution as to the future in my mind. Throughout the summer I played with time as a kitten tangles yarn, hoping that when the time came to do something the decision would be there.

To my mother my indecision spelled something like an agony. Knowing her only child as she did, she felt that at the last minute I would announce myself as "going to college" and that would be a minor catastrophe without suitable clothing prepared. Immediately after my graduation Mom began to wrest a wardrobe from yards of corduroy, flannel, ribbon, and taffeta. She, at least, was not going to be caught unprepared this time. And while my mother was trying to decide color and fashion, I was trying to decide my future. College sounded good to me. Drama was beginning to crystallize as a possible solution, and it certainly wouldn't do any harm to get a little polishing off at college while I learned the "know-how" of acting. After that I would be really ready to study under the direction of the Cecil B. DeMille that I hoped to find made to order when I was ready for the stage or radio.

I was a passionate bicyclist and early morning found me taking the wheel and the air. Usually I went to seven o'clock Mass by way of the lake-shore drive, and I became so accustomed to its beauties that the trip became my special opportunity to talk to God about all the things that I had to say. Often I would ask Him what He thought of my chances of getting under a good drama director, and I often prayed that He would see that I would be booked with the best. It must be someone who would be able to take me in hand and show me how to act any role that might come my way, whether "bit" part or "hit" part. I wanted to have the secret of catching the thrill of the dramatic moment and bringing that finger-tip awareness to others. I knew instinctively that this was demanding much but I knew, too, that it would be the only way to master the art form.

Deep down I felt that a good director must also possess the mark of true Franciscanism — lighthearted joy. My parents are Franciscans in the real meaning of the word. Everything they have is at God's service (and their neighbors') at all times with a smile and a prayer. This is the reason why our home has always been the general meeting place of all and sundry and why there is "open house" every night. Mom and Dad jokingly blame the fireplace as the center of attraction, but summer leaves them without a semblance of an excuse other than a well-filled cookie jar and pleasant lawn chairs. Yet there are always so many of the neighborhood kids about the house that Dad says he has to be careful where he walks so that he doesn't step on any "little people." Nor is it only the small fry that seek the little white house with the iron knocker. As a child I knew that deep, grown-up consultations took place occasionally. These were usually followed by a trip downtown which meant an ice cream cone or bag of candy for me but to Mom and Dad meant withdrawing their savings from the bank or placing a mortgage on the house to help a brother in a pinch. Years of such openhanded and openhearted generosity had made their charity and renunciation seem spontaneous and effortless. Theirs is a sure-fire imitation of the Giver of Galilee.

So passed a wonderful summer — packed with picnics, airplane rides, swimming, boating, and the million things a high school graduate who is too young to get a job might do to keep out of mischief. Apparently I wasn't thinking any more than my bicycle, yet that query pricked the edge of my consciousness: "My God, what do You want me to do?" And still I just didn't know.

And then one night in early September while I was making a holy hour in my room and watching the wick of the vigil light melt itself into tiny metallic balls and drop into the liquid wax, the old question came to the surface of my consciousness dragging behind it some further thoughts which like the wick rolled themselves into little answer balls and dropped deep into my soul. If I would be satisfied with no one but the best, then that director could be no other than God Himself. And yet, perhaps it was irreverent to think of Him as a director — but my catechism had always told me to pray to Him for *guidance* and *direction,* and I had been doing that for a long, long time. The tremendous consequences following this idea almost made me breathless as they lined themselves up one by one in parade fashion. I remembered that a priest had once said it was a very easy thing for religious to know the will of God because it was manifest in the commands and directives of superiors. Thus God's will is made known down to the least thing concerning one's living and acting. Acting — to play the role of God's leading lady.

Oh heavens! I wasn't worthy of such a part but that wasn't the real question. The real question was, "What does God want?" and I was becoming more aware every minute that perhaps He wanted me to be a nun. Nun — fettered to God by three vows: poverty, chastity, and obedience. Poverty — an assurance and an endeavor to travel light in order that one's trunk and heart be not too burdened to take to the rails if the next booking of the troupe demanded that. Chastity — free from personal ties but warmed by an intense and joyful love of all because each service performed for a neighbor is offered to the Lover Christ who has placed a smile upon every saint's lips and heart. Obedience — God the Director carefully training and blocking the acting right down to the least detail in order to ensure continual perfection in the one acting — the nun, His leading lady. So my question had gravitated right back to beginnings and the circle of thought that it formed cast a loop around divinity and at once I knew that the loop held not only God but also my soul. I knew what God wanted!

All that I had to do was join a troupe of Franciscans. Well, not quite all, because I still had to tell my parents.

I determined to cast my hand grenade of new-found decision into the middle of the dinner conversation the very next day. When Mom and Dad spoke about school opening for the fall term I realized that the zero hour had come.

I began casually, "I just decided . . ."

Mother intercepted eagerly, "See, I knew that you would decide to go to college after all. Well, I'm surely happy that I have your wardrobe well in hand."

After gulping hard I managed to squeak, "Well, that isn't exactly what I was going to say. I'm going to the convent."

Complete silence held the room taut for at least two minutes in which I could almost feel the alpha particles radiate from the atomic bomb my grenade turned out to be. However, there was another and vaster radiation going on. That was the radiation of God's grace. He was asking them to give Him a more thorough and rapid renunciation than they had ever given to their fellow men; He was giving them strength to do it with the graciousness with which they had always met every appeal.

Mother was the first to speak and quietly asked, "When do you have to be there?"

No doubt her mind had already accepted it and she was figuring out how quickly she could secure the list of clothes that most convents advise.

"Tomorrow!"

"TOMORROW!" Mom and Dad were taken aback. "Isn't this all rather sudden? Are you really sure that you know what you want?"

"Well, I wasn't sure until last night, but now I am convinced that God wants me to be a nun. So I dug up that literature that the sisters gave me last spring and it says that entrance days are from September second to fourth. Today is the third."

As soon as I said that I was sure it was God's will, both

Mom and Dad set about getting preparations accomplished for the trip. Daddy had only time to call the office and tell them he would not be at work in the morning because he was driving to La Crosse. And Mom had only time to pull out two of her new towels and dig into the college wardrobe to pull out the pair of black oxfords purchased for hiking. After much hurry and a desperate attempt to pack what I obviously did not have, both Mom and I managed a laugh because my whole wardrobe consisted of exactly two turkish towels and a pair of shoes.

"I'm afraid that they will have to outfit you there!" Mom smiled, a little crestfallen that she had once more been caught unprepared at the last minute as she had feared.

Soon, however, the house quieted down as each of the three of us tried to make the others believe that he or she was sleeping. In reality we were all pretty much on the ball — thinking. Although the shock and suddenness gave a slight anesthesia, still way down deep there was a terrible ripping pain. For me it was the first time that I was leaving my wonderful parents; for them it was giving back to God their only child whom they had received from Him what seemed like such a short time ago. Only God could have given them the strength needed at that moment and all the accumulated moments since in which they have so wholeheartedly and Franciscanly given their daughter to Him. In one stroke with lifelong implications they were more generous with God than with all others.

And so late the next afternoon Mom, Dad, and I were sitting in the parlor of St. Rose Convent waiting for the Mistress of Postulants. I had quite definitely embarked on my lifework of being a Franciscan troubadour. . . .

The thirteen years that have passed since that warm September afternoon have been years filled to the brim with love, joy, activity, and God. Beyond my most daring dream God has taken over the direction of my acting. There were three years of concentrated training during the postulancy and novitiate and since then God has continued His interest in me. He still minutely directs my life through superiors, and I have the gay security of knowing that I am doing just exactly what He wants. There have been many roles: student analyzing $KCLO_3$ or the poetry of T. S. Eliot; housekeeper wielding the potato peeler and broom; mother to the tiny tot who cannot button his coat or find his rubber; teacher to the wild adolescent with the dream of the future in his mind and the hieroglyphics of the past in his writing; friend to the youngsters who tamper with my initials reducing them from SML to SMILEY; and above all and through it all, stand-in for Genesius and Francis learning from the Head Director how to "become all things to all men" with a smile and a prayer.

JUST AS I AM

SISTER LORRAINE MARIE, S.S.A.[1]

THE faint ray of light from the living-room window pink-tinted the falling snowflakes as I trudged up the path. They were alone! Just as I had planned! Softly, I closed the kitchen door behind me and, in my mind's eye, visualized the scene. Dad reading his newspaper; Mother knitting as if her life depended upon the completion of someone's socks this very night or, perhaps, was it some lucky baby's sweater! I drew a quick breath. It was tonight . . . it had to be! I whispered a frightened little prayer and went in.

"Home already, Dot?" asked Mother in surprise, for it was unlike me to come in before eight-thirty at least when I worked in the parish library.

"Yes, Mom, I left Eve with Sue and came home to . . ." I could feel my heart thumping noisily and my throat felt parched and tight. "I want to talk to Dad and you about some-

---

[1] *Sister Lorraine Marie, a native of Central Falls, Rhode Island, entered the community of the Sisters of Saint Anne shortly after completing her high school course. This community, whose mother house is in Lachine, Quebec, is engaged mainly in teaching and has establishments in New England and in the Province of Quebec. Its members also conduct hospitals in British Columbia and are working in the mission fields of Alaska and Haiti. Sister Lorraine Marie now teaches at Saint Anne Academy, Marlborough, Massachusetts.*

thing . . . something important," I said, in what sounded to
me like someone else's voice.

"What is it, little girl?" Dad was all attention now. He
was an "angel" in the common bobby-sox parlance of the day,
and we all knew, Bob and Sis and I, that we meant more
to him than all the news in the country.

"Well, you see, Mom and Dad . . ." I tried to sound
businesslike and calm, ". . . in five months I'll be graduated
from high school and I must think of the future. I know that
you're willing to sacrifice much to send me to college and I
do appreciate it, but I'd like something better than that. I . . . I
want to be a nun!" I finished breathlessly.

It was as if a bombshell had struck the room. The silence
which followed was heavy with unspoken words. Mom's knitting hung limply in her stilled fingers, and Dad's evening
paper glided noiselessly to the floor. I dared not look into
their faces, yet I felt their piercing scrutiny. An agony of fear
gripped my heart and beads of perspiration stood on my forehead. I kept my eyes riveted on the silver-rose lamp by the
window, clasping and unclasping my hands nervously. For
a minute which lasted a seeming eternity, the silence was
unbroken. Hot tears welled up in my eyes which I closed
tightly so that only two trickled their normal course down my
cheeks. I was glad of that, for the next instant the door burst
open and Bob, looking like a veritable snowman, tramped in.

"Hello, folks. Real storm coming up. It's snowing harder
than ever. But wait till I tell you . . ." And out he launched
on the story of the latest hockey game of which he was, of
course, the star, second to none except, perhaps, the big senior
Joe Gendron.

I knew it was useless now. "What does a mere sophomore
understand about really important conversations, or psychologi-
cal moments, or momentous decisions or . . . anything except
baseball, football, and hockey?" I asked myself half angrily
as I retreated to my room. Far into the night I lay awake

watching the snowflakes silently bury my dreams, yet desperately hoping that the door would open to admit Mother carrying a cup of hot chocolate and coming to say that all was right.

The six o'clock alarm woke me from a troubled sleep. I really needed Mass today, and besides, I loved the short two-minute walk up Summit Hill with Dad on his way to work. We had grown so close in these daily chats which always ended in a quick hug and kiss at the corner. But Dad was already dressed to leave this morning and, looking out the window, not once at me, he said: "Got to go right away or I may miss the bus. It's tough walking."

My heart almost stopped in sheer disappointment, for I was sure he wanted to evade last night's issue. This could only mean that Mother had opposed my request and if she had, then I could understand his mute acquiescence in her decision. We had almost lost her, not quite six months ago, and never could anything have made us realize more fully how very precious she was. And too, she was still an invalid, and it would be a long time before she would be really well. She relied on me so much, almost too much. She had grown accustomed to consulting her eldest about every detail concerning the household but especially, yes especially, about the whims and fancies of dear old Grandfather.

Grandfather was a choleric old gentleman who thought his seventy-four years, his bad heart, and his iron will warranted all the activities of someone twenty years his junior. Frequently, on a pleasant day, he slipped away unnoticed, drove some fifty miles and returned home any time between four and ten P.M., and all this without a word as to his probable destination. The only signs of his absence were a vacant place at the dinner table and an empty garage. All of us knew that the doctor had forbidden him the use of the automobile, but nothing could weaken his determination. He was well and that was that! Since Grandmother's death twenty months earlier, we had used every conceivable argument to persuade him to live with us

instead of alone in the empty, cheerless rooms now bereft of
the quiet presence of the loved one who had been the sunshine
of his life. Even to my earnest pleadings he remained adamant,
and this was surprising enough for he usually ceded to me,
who could boast of the enviable honor of being his favorite.

At any rate, I was invaluable in most cases when it came
to managing Grandfather and his caprices. Consequently, this
and a dozen other perfectly valid reasons all militated against
my proposed departure for the novitiate.

When, two days later, I again summoned up enough courage
to speak to Mother of the matter uppermost in our minds, I
knew that the "No!" was final, for this year at least, and
that nothing short of a miracle would change it. Her words,
kind but firm, echoed and re-echoed in my ears for days. I
pondered over her arguments, weighed them, examined them
from every angle, and refuted them one by one. It all seemed
so very clear to me. The indecision with which, for the past
several months, I had considered the possibility of a religious
vocation, had vanished without a trace and left in its wake
only an undeniable certainty concerning the path I must
choose, and an indomitable will to overcome all obstacles to
my following it. I *had* to be a sister, not in two or three or
five years, for that would be *never*. God was calling me *now*.

Today, as I cast a retrospective glance upon the weeks of
ardent prayer and useless begging that followed, I realize that
God was strengthening my vocation. Opposition only made me
more determined, difficulty gave me a deeper appreciation of
the life I sought to lead, and contradiction prepared my will
to meet the still greater struggles of years to come. Nothing
mattered any longer, not even the dream of college that I
had been fostering; nothing made any difference except obtaining that all-important, absolutely necessary permission. And
by the time Graduation Day dawned I had it!

The victory was one of prayer with more than a wee bit
of the glory for Father Tom. When I had broached the subject

to him, he had asked rather curtly, "Why do you wish to be a nun?"

"Why, Father, I . . ." I stammered, feeling most uncomfortable under his steady, searching gaze and trying to clothe my reasons in suitable words that just would not come. "I don't really know . . . I have always wanted to, I guess," I added rather lamely.

But that was true. The thought that some day I should be a nun had been in my mind from as far back as I could remember. That desire had always lain deep within my heart, and the vague sense that I really would enter the convent had made most of my dreams about the future center round that hope. I had come to love the sisters, to admire their selfless devotion and their patient understanding and, as I grew to know them better, I became aware of a hidden force behind their lives of sacrifice, a secret source of strength which seemed to dispel anxiety and make problems disappear simply by confiding them to these women who always found the word of comfort and the healing balm for troubles big and small. The service of God and the salvation of souls, particularly the innocent souls of bright-eyed little children so avid of divine truth and light and beauty, held a deeper meaning for them than worldlings could conceive and, from it, they drew the undefinable happiness which radiated from their very contact. The world was certainly a better place to live in because of them, and I longed to penetrate their inner sanctum, to break down the real if invisible barrier which separated them from me. Truly, I wished to be a nun, to be His alone, *just as I am.*

It is true that, like so many other teen-agers, I had tried to shake off this obstinate desire — unsuccessfully, thank God. I rarely missed a party, and I could be counted on to be on hand for every picnic, excursion, or other festive occasion. I really enjoyed social gatherings. But the persistent thought that God was calling me had the queerest way of popping up at the most unexpected moments.

Here is an example of what I mean. Four of us had gone
to New York to attend the Summer School of Catholic Action
at Fordham University. We were determined to see and enjoy
all the better side of the metropolis. Amid the gay throng
crowding the broad sidewalks of brilliant Times Square, after
a most delightful evening at the Radio City Ice Show, suddenly and for no apparent reason, I felt an irresistible urge
to get away, to flee from all this useless confusion, deafening
noise, and unavailing pleasure-seeking, and to find refuge
within the cool, peaceful, prayerful walls of a cloister. The
impression lasted but a few minutes but I have never quite
forgotten it, nor have I ever been able to lose the sense of
peace and profound contentment which, thereafter, always
seemed to hover about a convent. Yes, ever afterward, when
I passed the sisters' home in the evening and saw only darkened
windows silvered by moonlight, my whole being longed to
become one of those chosen souls.

All of these thoughts flitted, in an instant, through my mind,
but my tongue refused to voice them. The priest would surely
think me silly or sentimental — which was exactly what I was,
I suppose. But does not every adolescent girl love a touch of
the romantic in whatever dream for the future is hers?

And so I answered hesitatingly, "I don't really know *why*,
Father. I feel that God is calling me and, more than anything
else in the world, I want to be His bride. Please don't think,
as Mother does, that I have been influenced. This is my own
free choice."

Father Tom seemed satisfied with the genuine desire that
animated me. He believed in my vocation. When I spoke
about opposition his advice was laconic. "How about consulting
the Master? He will win you if He really wants you. Always
go to Him. We humans, even the best of us, are but weak
instruments in His all-powerful hands."

Reassured and confident that ultimate victory would be mine,
I prayed as never before. Less than a month later I obtained

the coveted consent of my parents, and my hopes soared to the skies. I suspect that Father Tom had been quite an eloquent intercessor even if he was only the "weak instrument" of almighty God.

The days passed quickly. There were a hundred things to do, to make, to buy, before I should be ready. Never once did Mother renew her pleadings, but her saddened countenance wore a look of silent reproach which said more eloquently than words could have done, "Why so soon? Could you not stay with me one more year?" Outwardly she seemed not to understand my apparently unreasonable tenacity, but inwardly her lively spirit of faith had breathed a *fiat* of heroic acceptance of God's will. Still, it was heart-rending to see the unbidden tears stream down her face as we both sat in a cozy corner of the porch, the summer quiet broken only by the murmur of Dad's radio in the living room. There were new strands of silver in her chestnut hair, and the temptation often beset me to abandon every cherished dream for the sake of this one love.

It was July 31, the eve of my departure. As I gazed lingeringly about my little bedroom by the rosy glow of the dainty lamp, I found everything beautiful and dear — the peach-pink wallpaper with its blue forget-me-nots, Sister's big panda sitting primly in the corner, and the exquisite statuette of God's Mother in its niche of ivory. I had often envied other girls their bedrooms, which seemed so much more modern and attractive, but on this particular evening none could rival mine.

I arose next morning with a strange lump in my throat, which seemed to increase in size with every hour. I could hardly eat because of it, even the favorite dishes Mom had prepared especially for me. All afternoon relatives and friends dropped in to say good-by, many bringing sweets to eat or literature to read on the long trip to Montreal. Each farewell was another note in the melody in a minor key that filled my last day at home. I experienced the truth of the well-known French maxim, "Partir, c'est mourir un peu." Finally, after a sobbing good-by from Sis and a manly hug from Bob, I boarded the train with Dad's tear still on my cheek and the piercing memory of Mother's brave farewell. It would have been much easier to bear a flood of tears than her restrained, loving, infinitely sad last kiss. As the train passed home, I waved to Grandfather with the indefinite feeling that he would no longer be among us when the family and I met again.

Two golden years in the novitiate revealed to me the depths of love I never could have fathomed. I say "golden" years because the remembrance I have of them is one of radiant happiness. I have forgotten the poignant hours of loneliness, the fleeting moments of regret for things once mine, and the times of anguish when doubt concerning my vocation blotted out the light. Yes, they are forgotten in the peaceful joy that pervaded every hour, even the most difficult, of those two blessed years.

On Profession Day, as I knelt before the altar and vowed undying love, love set free by the very fetters of poverty, chastity, and obedience, every event of my whole life seemed but a link in the chain which had brought me to the supreme realization of this day's tremendous sacrifice. Sacrifice it was, I well knew, but a joyous, loving sacrifice — and a complete sacrifice. Why had I come three hundred miles from home, here among strangers? "Why" was no longer a mystery. He had wanted me, called me, *just as I am,* a frail, faltering, imperfect creature. He had pursued my wavering soul, had whispered pleadingly:

> Rise, clasp My hand and come!
> Ah! fondest, blindest, weakest,
> I am He whom thou seekest!

My twenty years were all His, only His, the youthful springtime of my life. With Mother Mary my soul thrilled an ecstatic *Magnificat* for all the bounties of the Lord.

Almost four years had elapsed since my first consecration when Mother and Dad, this time beaming, presented me with the simple silver band, symbol of the irrevocable yes of perpetual vows. Even then Dad said, "The door at home is open wide, little girl, if you have not found the happiness you sought." There was a wistful longing in his voice which bespoke the emptiness of those years. Yet, I knew that my parents' hearts were overflowing with gratitude that the King of Angels had chosen their own daughter for His spouse. Mother said, her gray eyes shining, "We're so proud of you."

Tonight is Christmas Eve. As I sit here reminiscing, the December sky twinkles with a million diamond stars, and the slender sickle of a moon brightens the long white rows of little girls' beds — empty beds now, for the resident students have gone home for the holidays. In a few, a very few minutes, chimes from everywhere will rend the peaceful night with their immortally glorious "Noel." "Joy to the world, the Lord is come!" And in a few minutes at Midnight Mass within the cloistered walls of my convent home, veiled heads will bow in homage to their King and their God. He is the center, the all of our lives, this tiny Babe of Bethlehem. In a few moments, *just as we are,* we shall enfold Him, this God of Love, in the sublime embrace of Holy Communion. He has beckoned us to follow Him *just as we are.* He loves us *just as we are.* One day, soon perhaps, or later, He will take us home with Him *just as we are.* For the holy joy which fills our hearts this Christmas night is but a faint foretaste of the incommensurable happiness of seeing Him, the Beloved of consecrated souls, in the ineffable splendor of a Christmas in heaven.

KINDLY LIGHT

SISTER M. MARISTELLE, O.S.B.[1]

I LEFT the chapel to light the candles for "Mass" just as the community was finishing Prime. A last look assured me that everything was in readiness; then I slipped downstairs to call a taxi. "Come as soon as possible," I ordered.

The whole house, this house where I had found happiness and contentment in the companionship of holy women, was silent. The sisters were all in chapel. In a few minutes my cab pulled up, and with the two light suitcases I had packed in haste and left in readiness the night before, I climbed in and directed the driver to take me to the depot. A new, strange life opened before me, and I felt insecure, indeed, as I faced it utterly alone, knowing only that my conscience was certain; that I must, whatever the anguish of separation, become a Catholic at least.

As the cab rolled on, I glanced in reminiscence over the steps that had brought me to this decision. I had always been attracted to sisters. I remembered waiting for the Catholic nuns to pass by our house in my pre-school days, because they

---

[1] *Sister Maristelle is a convert who had the unique experience of leaving the Anglican Sisters of St. Mary, becoming a Catholic, and entering a Benedictine convent all on the same day. At present Sister Maristelle is teaching in St. Symphorosa School, in Chicago. The mother house of her Benedictine community is at the Convent at St. Scholastica, 7430 Ridge Avenue, Chicago 45, Illinois.*

always had a kind word and a piece of candy for me. We lived in a small town in northern Michigan. Dad was a Lutheran, and Mother, nominally an Episcopalian. Because we didn't like the Lutheran church where the services were all in German, we soon followed our mother's religion. When I was older we moved to another town and, except for an occasional visit with friends of different denominations, my attendance at church was very irregular. Curiously enough, I felt a tremendous interest in the Dominican nuns who taught at a Catholic parish nearby.

When I was nineteen, I was in a serious car accident which incapacitated me for a long time. This gave me a chance to do a lot of reading and thinking. I wanted to be a nun. I didn't know how to go about it, though, and I had about made up my mind to ask advice of the Dominicans when I read about the Episcopalian Sisters who taught at Kemper Hall School in Kenosha, Wisconsin. I wrote to the superior, who sent a gracious reply inviting me to come to Chicago at any time to get acquainted with her sisters there. My parents, I knew, would not be favorable to my desire for religious life, though I was a bit more hopeful of their consent now that I had found a group of Protestant sisters I could join. However, I wanted at all costs to avoid hurting them, so I took no further steps until I was twenty-one. Then I told my father and mother that I wanted to go to Chicago, and they agreed. I left home on the day after Thanksgiving dinner in 1921, with their blessing and approval.

What my family did not know was that I had informed the superior of the Anglican Congregation of St. Mary of my plans to enter her order, if she would accept me. Mother Mary Sylvia was gracious enough to come from Kenosha to Chicago to meet me at the train. We went at once to St. Mary's Home, now Marillac Center, and at that time a home for young girls. I worked there for a few weeks with the six nuns who serviced the house. I had fallen in love with the sisters and felt attracted to the work they were doing. Accordingly, on February 1, Mother Mary Sylvia came to take me to Kenosha for the beginning of my novitiate. On the following day, the patronal feast of the congregation, I received the postulant's uniform and began my training for the Anglican Sisterhood. This was a new, beautiful world, and I entered into it with a full heart. The sisters led a fervent prayer-life, singing the Divine Office most beautifully in the vernacular. There were daily "Mass" and opportunity for weekly "confession." We had classes in religious life, church history, and Gregorian chant from a mistress who was a fine, intelligent woman. On August 24 I received the habit of the community and the name Sister Mary Isabel; my two years' novitiate had begun.

After the completion of my first year of novitiate training, I was permitted to go to my home for a visit. It was customary for each sister to have a full month's rest and change in the summertime. My parents found it hard to understand my attraction for this new life, and I must have seemed strange and distant to them. When I had informed them of my real motives for leaving home, they had telegraphed me to come home at once and not to do anything so foolish; and now here I was back, wearing a habit and following a rule of life that they had no background for comprehending. After ten days I was glad, indeed, to return to my convent, and I know that my stay brought sadness to those I loved. It was a hard realization, but I soon became engrossed in my new life and left my parents' reactions to God. When I was called back the following year, I found my mother ill and unable to do her household work. There were eight young children, and my father asked me to remain at home to care for them until my mother's recovery. Selfishly, perhaps, I refused and returned to Kenosha, but for the first time I was not at peace, restless in the thought that my duty lay elsewhere. Another circumstance added to my spiritual confusion. Though I had the good sense to realize that, inadvertently, she was spoiling me, I couldn't help reveling in the high favor shown me by my immediate superior. I knew that I had not come to religious life for this. Finally, convinced that my family needed me desperately, I left the mother house and returned home. With my profession imminent, this move certainly cost me much.

Ironically, I became sick myself after a few weeks, and the doctor prescribed rest and change. I wrote to my superior of my difficulties. She advised against my returning until I had a year to recuperate and suggested a place in the home of one of the sisters where I could be companion to an aged relative. I had been there only a few months when my charge, a dear old lady, died, and I was left without employment. There were plenty of positions in nearby New York, and I began work in the science department of Parke-Davis in a clerical capacity.

New York was wonderful. I loved the excitement of big city life; my work was pleasant, and my big, redheaded boss, a doctor, was the kindest of employers. I made friends, one thing led to another, and soon an attractive opportunity for marriage offered itself. Just at this juncture Mother Mary Sylvia wrote to say that she was coming to the order's mother house in Peekskill. She would be glad to see me, if I cared to visit. This seemed providential, and in the interview which followed I talked things over thoroughly with her. With two states of life presenting an attractive picture, I was in a dilemma, and I needed objective help to decide between them.

"Continue just as you have been," advised Mother, after she heard my story, "and come back in a few weeks. In the meantime pray and think things over some more. I'll do the same." I followed her advice, and the following September found me back at our Kenosha mother house with scarcely a regret for the prospects that had seemed so alluring. It meant beginning my novitiate all over, but it seemed a happy home-coming to me.

On September 18, 1926, I made my perpetual vows in the

Anglican Congregation of St. Mary — vows so sacred and solemn in the sight of God, and recognized as such by His true Church, that a papal dispensation was required when later I wished to be released from them. I was at peace and settled down to the work of the community. I admired and loved my companions, women truly striving for spiritual perfection. The co-operation and charity in the house were gratifying, and there was a sincere spirit of silence and prayer. Oddly enough, most of the community's spiritual reading was from Catholic authors. Cardinal Newman and Mother Janet Stuart were my constant companions at this time. Slowly, surely, under the influence of these holy authors, I began to arrive at a frightening conviction, all the more disturbing since I was so thoroughly in love with my community. I was in the wrong Church; I must become a Catholic.

My anguish at the thought of another important and irrevocable decision was heightened by the grief I must cause our Mother General, with whom I had formed a deep spiritual friendship. As a final profession gift I had been allowed to accompany this religious on a visitation trip to one of our houses in Davenport, Iowa. Though we were together for only two short weeks, we grew very close. I looked upon her as a sure spiritual guide and a particularly understanding friend. Deeply prayerful, nourishing her interior life almost exclusively on St. Teresa and St. John of the Cross, she gave me in her frequent letters the guidance and direction that have been a permanently inspiring force in my life. However, discerning though she was, I knew it would be impossible to persuade her of the wisdom of my decision to become a Catholic, as some time previously she had told me that one of the greatest trials she had ever endured occurred when a dearly loved superior and another sister she had known had left the community to become Roman Catholics. Not only was she unable to understand this move on their part, but she regarded it as a defection from a life vowed to God. She had dwelt on the anguish it caused her. Harassed at the thought that my leaving must cause her another poignant sorrow, I tried to put the growing assurance out of my mind, and for some time I was successful.

One day I went with a group of sisters from my house to a Carmelite convent in the city where I was stationed. As I prayed before the statue of St. Theresa, my "attraction to Rome" suddenly returned. I recommended the matter to her, told her to show me what to do about it, and straightway forgot the incident.

St. Theresa was not so remiss. In the summer of 1932, I was sent to the mother house of the order at Peekskill for a retreat and summer vacation. Facing Bear Mountain on a bluff rising from the banks of the blue Hudson, the mother house was restful for body and soul. My dear friend had completed her tenth year as Mother General and was now free of office. Often in the afternoon after the end of the time for silence, we walked along the river path, and I listened to the wise words of this beautiful soul. It was a time of joy and peace, the lull before a frightening spiritual storm.

In the following school term in Chicago I became conscious of a growing repugnance in teaching some sections of the Anglican catechism. Worse, I was obsessed by the increasing conviction that the Real Presence was not in our chapel, that I was not receiving the true Body and Blood of Christ in Holy Communion each morning. The reading I did to enlighten myself increased my anxiety on these points. Pleadingly, I began a novena to the Little Flower. The fruit of my prayer was the absolute certainty that I must become a Catholic. From this time I began to look for ways and means to carry out my desire. On a trip to the downtown district, I happened to be left alone while my superior, who had accompanied me, went on to complete an errand. I went directly to the Chancery Office, and asked to see a priest. Father Hayes soon arrived, and I told him, rather incoherently, I am afraid, that I wanted to be a Catholic but did not want to leave the community to which I now belonged. I would have to enter a religious order at once, as I had no desire to return to the world after eleven years in the convent. Father found I was quite well grounded in the essentials of the Catholic Faith. My extensive reading had proved of real help to me. My explanation as to why I felt I had a call to become a Catholic convinced him, and he said I must follow my conscience. To my great relief he volunteered to look around for a community that would be suitable to a person of my unusual background. My only stipulation was that I enter a community which sang the Divine Office.

Father Hayes advised me to return to my convent until affairs could be arranged. In the meantime I could get in touch with him at any time. This I was often able to do, since I frequently had permission to read and study at the library. Before too long Father told me he had found the place for me. It was with the Benedictine Sisters of St. Scholastica Convent in Chicago. The Divine Office was an important part of the spiritual life of these nuns, and the superior had consented to receive me. In an interview with her, it was decided that I should leave to come to St. Scholastica at my first opportunity.

Now that the break was at hand and all the arrangements were completed, my repugnance at the thought of leaving my convent increased fourfold. I prayed again to the Little Flower, and that night when I was retiring, my doubts disappeared. I would do this thing, and now. I straightened all my effects and packed what I would need in two small bags, which I placed in readiness in the front vestibule. Then I composed a note to my superior which I left on my desk in plain sight. I could not have faced a leave-taking, with the certainty that my motives would not be understood, that I could not hope for this understanding even from the sister I most loved and revered in this community. This was the better way,

I thought, and easier for all concerned. Then I slept in peace.

At ten o'clock the next morning I was conditionally baptized in the Chancery chapel in Chicago. Unfortunately, I had taken breakfast downtown, so that I could not receive my First Holy Communion, but I went to confession. Then Father Hayes had me driven to one of the convents of my new community, where I changed from the habit of the Anglican Sisters of St. Mary to the black uniform of a Benedictine postulant. My quest for truth had ended.

Today I look back over many years of life as a professed Catholic religious. I am now teaching in an elementary school in Chicago. My childhood dream of being a sister is fulfilled, and with God's grace and in the company of my fellow sisters, I am doing a work which has always been dear to my heart. As I recall the steps which have led to this culmination, I can see clearly the sure, firm guidance of God unmistakably revealing His holy will in my regard, gently fulfilling His eternal designs in the many vicissitudes of my life.

PEARL FOR A DIAMOND

SISTER ELIZABETH ANN, O.L.V.M.[1]

"MARY, you don't mean it."

"But I do. I've always wanted to and I'm going in September."

"Five months from now! But I don't see why . . ."

My sister had just told me that she intended to enter the convent. Certainly I knew that girls did such things, but my own sister! It just didn't seem right. She was a freshman in college now, and I, three years younger, appreciated her as I never had before. Why should she spoil everything by going to a convent?

No amount of argument on my part during the next few months was able to make the least impression. Off to the convent she went, still leaving me unconvinced as to the wisdom of such a step.

Four years later I followed her, but not to the same convent. She was a teaching sister; I wished to be a missionary. Unlike hers, my vocation was a "whirlwind affair."

It was bad enough, I thought, for my sister to enter. That

---

[1] *Sister Elizabeth Ann was born in Chillicothe, Ohio. During the retreat in her sophomore year in college she decided to become a missionary. She did not go to distant shores, however, but entered Our Lady of Victory Missionary Sisters, whose mother house is at Victory Noll, Huntington, Indiana. This community offers its members countless opportunities for doing missionary work in the United States.*

I should do so never occurred to me, not even in my wildest imaginings. Nor did it occur to anyone else either. Not one sister ever mentioned religious vocation to me. The sisters were not given to "talk vocation" to this girl or that, but it happened sometimes, and rightly, that if they thought a girl had the signs of a vocation (it was a boarding school and certainly they had every opportunity to observe their girls), they prudently questioned her as to her plans in life. I can remember only one occasion when our chaplain asked me what I intended to do in the future. It was just a routine question, I'm sure, put to all the seniors in high school.

I answered, "Get married, I suppose, Father."

Now I of course had no marriage plans, but it was sort of a case of elimination. I was sure the religious life was not for me, so what else could I answer?

All this was up until my sophomore year in college. In the fall, shortly after school began, I received a letter from home. Some good friends of ours lived in the city not far from where our college was located. Now the oldest son, a Jesuit, ordained the year before, was leaving for India and I was supposed to visit the family. My mother could not go, so it became my duty, etc. I could imagine nothing worse. In the first place, I had never met the priest. His sisters had often visited us, and I had many times visited at his home, but he was never there. Jesuits studied so long! I would have to go the following Sunday, for Father was to leave for New York Monday morning. It would be something like visiting a funeral parlor.

But there was no getting out of it. Well, I would go, but not alone. I asked Marge to go with me. She was a senior from my home town and she had met Father's sisters when they visited us. So dutifully we paid our call, arriving around four in the afternoon. The young Jesuit was out at Mercy Convent saying good-by to his three sisters there. Of course, we had to wait. Besides, we were immediately invited to have supper with them.

Now, it was a big family, even without the three girls who were Sisters of Mercy. The married brothers and sisters were there with their children, and we made a big table. It was, besides, an extremely merry table. You would have thought it was just an ordinary but very happy family get-together instead of a farewell meal for the son who was leaving for the other side of the world, perhaps never to return. Father himself was the life of the party. After that, I think his mother was. We had a wonderful time.

When we left the table, the jolly conversation continued. The priest, with a little one on each knee, blew smoke rings around them, much to the delight of the children and the consternation of their mothers. I was politely asked to play the piano, and the time passed quickly for Marge and me. One of the boys drove us back to school.

We were in the college building only a little while when I had a phone call. It was the Jesuit, to tell me that I had left my ring on the piano. I thanked him and said not to bother sending it out, that I would stop for it the next Saturday.

The next morning at Mass I had an idea. I had been very much impressed by that visit the night before. Here were a priest and several scholastics (Father had told us about his companions on the journey) going off to India, giving up home and country to preach the Gospel. Not the least impressive was the generous attitude of the priest's own family at the sacrifice. Down in my heart I felt that I must do something, too. What it was, was not clear, but then came my wonderful idea. I tried a couple of Jesuit houses in the city before I reached Father. Then I timidly explained the reason for my call.

"Father, about that diamond ring. I wish you'd just take it with you."

Astonished silence for a few seconds at the other end of the line. Then — "Take it with me! What will I do with it?"

"Get some money for it in New York. It's worth a few hundred dollars. You can use the money, can't you?"

"Of course I can . . . but . . . well, I don't think I ought to take it. Maybe our Lord wants something else from you besides a diamond ring."

I hung up, very much disappointed. With the heedlessness of youth, it had not occurred to me that I should not give away diamond rings without asking my parents' permission. Besides, it was a sort of hand-me-down at that. It had been my sister's high school graduation present. Anyway, it was an awful anti-climax to have to claim the old ring the next Saturday. If the priest's mother knew anything about it, she did not let on.

During the winter I became more than just a dues-paying member of the Catholic Students Mission Crusade. I began to take an interest in the missions. We had our annual retreat that year the first three days of Holy Week. The retreat master told the story of St. Philip Neri and the ambitious young man. Each time he told St. Philip his high aspirations in this world, the saint would prod him on with "And then?" Only the retreat master always said it in Italian, *"E poi?"*

That is all I remember about the retreat, but it was enough. My mind was made up — just like that. Like the young man, I too must seek higher.

During our Easter vacation I told my mother quite bluntly that I wanted to be a missionary. She replied by telling me about Our Lady of Victory Missionary Sisters, known then as the Society of Missionary Catechists. She liked them because they were "all-American." She told me that she had always had great devotion to our Blessed Mother under the title of Our Lady of Victory and besides, she had always been a great admirer of Bishop Noll, who was sponsoring the new community and had built the mother house at Huntington, Indiana. She got *Our Sunday Visitor* and pointed out the column about the "Catechists." Then I wrote to a Jesuit friend of ours to tell him what I wanted and *he* mentioned the Victory Noll Sisters. In fact, he even wrote to Huntington and then sent me the interesting leaflets he received from there.

The vocation of a Victory Noll Sister appealed to me too, but I would not admit how much, right then and there. Human nature being what it is, I did not want anyone suggesting any particular community to me! But all the time I was sure this was just what I wanted. I knew positively I did not want to teach school. Many missionaries did. But here was a community whose principal work was teaching catechism. The sisters had to become specialists in it. Then they visited homes, especially the homes of the poor. They trained altar boys, choirs, conducted sodalities.

At that time their work was confined to New Mexico and California, but the stories I read in the *Missionary Catechist*, their monthly magazine, were thrilling indeed. It sounded adventurous and youth likes adventure. These sisters drove cars. Many sisters do now, but at that time it was unheard of. I liked their modern dark blue habit and veil. The habit was relieved by white collar and cuffs, and the veil by a white veil band. All these things I had read about, but I would like to see them for myself.

One of my friends, in whom I confided, lived at Logansport, Indiana, which is not very far from Huntington. Mary had practically made up her mind to enter the community of the sisters who taught us in school, but still she was interested in Victory Noll and knew that I was. So she suggested that I go home with her when school was out, and we would go up to Huntington for a visit. I was delighted.

When the news got around that I was going home with Mary, one of the girls asked cannily, "How many brothers does Mary have?" I do not remember exactly now, but there were at least four or five, all handsome boys, either still at Notre Dame or just graduated from there. Mary was a senior so they came en masse for commencement week activities, a couple of cousins with them for good measure. Mary was very popular that week.

My visit to Victory Noll decidedly clinched the matter. As soon as I stepped inside its doors, I knew I belonged. I made arrangements to enter in September. On the way home I had a few hours' wait at a station between trains and was met by one of my best friends and classmates. She told me that Bob, the boy in her crowd in whom she was most interested, was going to the Jesuit novitiate in September. I told her then what I intended to do. She cried, but I am sure I was not the only reason for her tears.

I can look back now on almost a quarter of a century of religious life. God has been very good to me. In the first place, perhaps because things happened so fast, I did not go through a period of indecision and turmoil and doubts as some girls do before and even for a time after they enter. The sisters at school, when they heard of my decision, were most helpful and did not try to dissuade me from entering a community other than their own, and a new one at that. My mother, although I found out only later how much she missed me, had been praying for my religious vocation and welcomed it when it came. My father never suggested that I stay home and help the family, in spite of his own illness and inability to work. My happiness was all that mattered to him. After the first flood of tears when my mother left me at Victory Noll, there was no homesickness. My superiors have always been most kind and considerate, and my companions have been real sisters to me through the years. I do not mean to imply that everything has been easy and delightful from the purely natural point of view. No, but I do say that what Christ gives a religious far outweighs the little she gives up for Him.

Among the memories of the years some are more vivid than others. Vow day for instance. Most sisters, no matter how far away their homes are, have relatives and friends with them on that day of days, but it so happened that I had no one.

My father was in his last illness and my mother could not leave him. It was on March 25, and my sister was teaching and could not come. Neither could my brother be with me, for he was in college. But it was better that way. I felt that I belonged more wholly to Him to whom I had vowed myself. First vows are always taken at our mother house. Perpetual vows might be made in one of our mission convent chapels. Some day I hope to visit again the tiny chapel in Nevada where I gave myself to our Lord for life. I often visit it in spirit.

To recount mission experiences would take a volume. Let me put high on the list the joy of baptizing a dying baby, a privilege that does not happen often. Then there is the ever new thrill of seeing the little ones I prepared receive our Lord in Holy Communion for the first time.

Nothing is so satisfying as instructing adult converts and then seeing the waters of baptism poured on their heads. Finding prospective converts is a thrill all its own. How often we meet them on our rounds of home visiting! I recall especially the woman who opened the door to us so eagerly and with tears in her eyes thanked us for coming. She heard we were in the neighborhood and was so afraid we would pass her by "because," she added, "I've made up my mind that I want to be a Catholic."

In this same town so many received the grace of conversion and so many lapsed Catholics returned to the practice of their religion that one man, himself a convert of ten years, suggested jokingly, "We either have to build a larger church or get rid of the sisters." We were only God's instruments, but it is a wonderful thing to know that He is using us to bring about the salvation of souls.

Precious are the memories of preparing for Holy Mass to be offered in a poor home on the Texas plains, or in a tiny one-room school, the celebrant using the teacher's desk for an altar, the congregation kneeling on the floor around him. Never will I forget a Christmas when we sang three High Masses, each one in mission places many, many miles apart.

Every missionary sister has such memories as these and others, too, of her own. And each one can answer as did one of our sisters when a little girl asked her if she gets *paid* for all the work she does. "Yes, Juanita," Sister answered, "God pays me."

GIVE THE BRIDE A VEIL

SISTER M. ANNUNCIATA, R.S.M.[1]

ANY years ago — never mind how many —
I was a little girl in a convent boarding
school. I wore pigtails and brown chambray skirts, which were
always too short because I was constantly growing out of
them. I was very studious, rather pious, and greatly interested
in what was going on around me. I thought the nuns, our
teachers, the loveliest people I had ever met, and more than
once it crossed my youthful mind that it were well to remain
among them always. This half-defined opinion I confided to
Sister Patricia, the Irish lay sister who gave us meals. She
was not too deeply moved.

Then one day something happened.

Because I had been reared in a rural section of the South
where my family were the only Catholics for miles around,
my social activities had been limited. In such areas, as you
may know, social life is closely linked with churchgoing. Any
compromise in that direction was sternly interdicted by my

---

[1] *Sister Annunciata, a native of Mississippi, is a Sister of Mercy
of the Union and a teacher at St. Francis Xavier Academy at
Vicksburg, Mississippi. The members of this community are engaged in teaching, nursing, other works of charity and missionary
activity at home and abroad. The Sisters of Mercy of the Union
have nine provinces in the United States. The address of their
general mother house is 9800 Kentsdale Drive, Bethesda, Washington 14, D. C.*

stanch Catholic father, which state of affairs threw my two
sisters, my one brother — and me — right back on our own
resources for amusement.

We *were* resourceful. We read a great deal; played with
imaginary children (don't call the psychiatrist!). We staged
plays; we even edited a family newspaper, *The Four Leaf
Clover*. Our pseudonyms were taken from Dickens' novels —
mine was Susan Nipper — and every type of literature flowed
from our ambitious pens. We played charades and entertained
at fancy dress balls, which the four guests were wont to attend
arrayed as characters from favorite books. At this my brother
sometimes drew the line.

It was a pleasant sort of life, but it left me a little one-sided.
Boarding school routine was just what I needed to round me
out. The girls there found me precocious, because I could use
long words and quote unending lines of poetry, but they had
many things to teach me, I assure you, about the ordinary
facts of life.

Among the normal experiences I had missed were weddings.
I had never seen one. True, I had read and savored the lovely
lines of Coleridge —

> The bride hath paced into the hall;
> Red as a rose is she;
> Nodding their heads before her goes
> The merry minstrelsy —

but I had never seen one of these blushing beauties pace, and
I was not at all sure of how the merry minstrelsy managed
their nodding heads, which brings me right back to the story
of my vocation.

One day the silence and decorum of our well-ordered school
was disrupted by the news that the boarders were invited to
a wedding. In St. Patrick's Church? *Yes.* Could we go? *Yes.*
All of us. *Certainly; it would do us good. Be ready and in
ranks at ten tomorrow.* (Oh, those ranks in which you walked

with the girl nearest your size, whether your tastes ran counter or parallel to hers!) Special seats would be reserved for us, students of St. Aloysius Academy. Excitement ran high throughout the day, and night brought fitful slumber. But at last the beautiful October morning dawned under those high blue skies that arch the hills and valleys of my native State. Long before ten o'clock we had assembled. I can see it all now and feel the ecstasy of it: the self-important altar boys lighting candles; the nervous pastor making useless trips from church to sacristy; the pompous ushers wielding power; and the excited girls around me trembling with the bated breath that precedes a climax.

Suddenly came a loud peal of the organ; the bridal procession was advancing! I strained forward. First, there was a youthful ring-bearer, supporting a silken cushion; then the pretty bridesmaids bedight in pastel shades and carrying roses; but I had no eyes for these. It was the bride that held me spellbound. The yards of satin train, the billowing veil, the tiny slippers, the radiant face lifting itself to that of the shy young groom (in tie and tails, which I had never seen before!). Truly if it be a sin to envy, I was the most offending soul alive. I heard the exhortation and the exchange of vows. Whether in the flesh or out of it, I knew not, I followed Mass. Then off again for the recessional, when I could gaze at the retreating bride; she was really pacing now.

It was over. My trance was ended. In perfect pairs we genuflected and left the church. The vulgar rice over which we stepped had no charm for me. Only the vision of the bride and groom swam before my eyes, shutting out all thought of reality — which included study, work, and play.

I was still projecting myself into the sentiments of the bride, leaning on her father's arm and pacing, when I encountered my friend, Sister Patricia.

"Oh, Sister!" I blurted out. "I've changed my mind. I'm not going to be a nun. I want to be a bride."

Sister Patricia was not nearly so disturbed as I had expected. She only clicked her teeth in her peculiar way and answered:

"Wait until you see a sister received into the convent. She is a bride, too, and wears a wreath and veil, but the Bridegroom is the good Lord Himself."

I stopped dead in my tracks. Bride? Groom? The sisters?

"But He isn't there," I faltered. "He doesn't take part, does He?"

"Yes, He *is* there, in the Blessed Sacrament; and the Bishop is there to represent Him and speak the words. You've seen nothing yet!" She actually sniffed.

I had no response; but I had some long, long thoughts, and for days to come I mulled them over. So that was it! These sisters were brides. This explained their calm, contented faces, their glowing eyes; that ageless look upon the forehead of Sister Columba, the old sick nun, whose skin was like ivory and whose blue-veined hands were as frail as the lace she endlessly tatted. This accounted, I deducted further, for their interest in and enthusiasm for little things. They were in love. They lived in a constant comradeship with Someone who was a lover. This was what was meant by a vocation!

The full impact of such a truth did not come upon me all at once. I hugged my secret, sharing it with no one, not even my secret pal. But days slipped into weeks, weeks into months, and deeper and deeper this beautiful thing entered into my soul and took possession of it: religious profession is marriage to Jesus.

When I moved into the teen-age group, the significance of such espousals took stronger hold upon me. You see, I had read widely for one so young. Thank God, I had read the best — good Catholic novels, as well as Scott and Thackeray and Dickens' "sweet unsullied page." I knew (I really did!) a great deal about love; and like all other girls of my age I wanted to love and to be loved like the beautiful Annabel Lee. Of course I did not know *everything* about love — who does? I did not know the full implications of the surrender entailed in all love, human and divine; but I doubt very seriously if any young girl realizes all that will be demanded of her and all that she will receive from her beloved, when she first accepts the rose of his devotion.

As the years went by and I learned more about the sisters, observing them as I did at close range, I saw their romance unfold before me. I became enamored of the idea of being a bride of Christ. I made no comparisons between Him and earthly lovers; such comparisons were not in order, it seemed, when human love had to be measured with that of God. What was really happening, I know now, was this: God had chosen me, and I thought I was choosing Him.

I cannot say that this mood was constant. For a year or more it came and went. There were periods when I did a deal of daydreaming (my early life had conditioned me for that). At times I envisioned myself as a famous actress, starring with the stage celebrities of my day; again as a noted writer, in great demand for lectures, particularly in boarding schools for girls. Sometimes I considered marriage and a family. But these intervals were short. In hours of prayer and quiet reflection my big discovery would rush in upon me and overwhelm me. To be a sister was to be a bride of Jesus, to exchange nuptial vows with Him, to enjoy His special affection in this world, and to follow Him in heaven with a song that only virgins sing.

In my freshman year of high school I made a retreat. For the first time I came face to face with the End of Man, the Use of Creatures, the Kingdom of Christ. After that the daydreams ceased. I knew what I wanted. I saw no need for waiting. It wasn't easy to tear at the strong, sweet ties that bound me to my family, but God's grace was there, as always. So without pomp or circumstance I entered the novitiate in July of my sixteenth year. What did I say? My arrival was devoid of circumstance, it is true, but not without its bit of pomp. Because of my tender age, the Mistress of Novices and pretty young Sister Aloysius were at the station to meet me. I, however, looking neither left nor right, alighted from the train, commandeered a carriage, and rode up to the convent behind a pair of prancing white horses. About twenty minutes later the Mistress and her companion arrived — on foot.

With this brave beginning I embarked upon my postulancy. The twenty-fifth of the following March was my bridal day. Sister Patricia had not deceived me. There were the shimmering gown, the flowing veil, the satin slippers. (I wore a *three*. Do they make that number now?) The Groom was there in the Blessed Sacrament, and the Bishop was there to "speak the words." He prayed that what God had begun in me He would Himself perfect, implying that if I stood the test of two years' novitiate, I would be married to Jesus forever.

An old, historic, and very delightful convent was my testing ground. The two years was a period of many joys and also of great trial, for my frail health threatened to disqualify me for Profession. Our Lady of Lourdes, however, came to my assistance, healing my body and moving my superiors, I do believe, to accept me.

It was a rich day in late August, my Vow Day. The summer sun had burned the leaves to crimson. I could see them through the window from my chapel stall. The flowers on the altar drooped with heat; the air was sweltering; but never a bride was nearer heaven than the little one prostrate on the chapel floor, while the choir struggled with the weather and the *Te Deum*. This at last was the day I had longed for. It reached out and touched eternity — for the slender ring on the third finger of my left hand kept telling me that I was espoused to Him whom angels serve and whose beauty the sun and moon admire. I belonged to Jesus, and no one could take me away.

I think you would like to know, now, how this marriage has lasted, how it has stood up under the years. Has it held the level of high romance, or has it broken down under the strain of monotonous living? I can answer that one. Because

I am a teacher and have never experienced two identical days in a row, I don't know the meaning of monotony. But to judge the durability of my romance, I ask you to look at any happily married couple in the world. What do you think has happened to their love over a period of time? Do you think anyone, even they themselves, can tell you how it has grown and deepened? When and where? Always, everywhere, silently and imperceptibly, their love has grown richer with knowledge, deeper with suffering.

Do you think your parents ever knew the depth of their affection for each other until they sat by your bedside through the long night watches, waiting for your fever to abate, or in some staggering sorrow gripped each other's hand in silent understanding? Happiness, too, has drawn them closer, obstacles surmounted, successes shared. Life together has welded their souls into one.

So it is with the divine romance — growth in knowledge and a quiet, steady advance in love. The bride of this union must suffer too, because her Spouse has suffered. She must share with Him her joys and sorrows, her triumphs and her failures; she must become one with Him in love.

When I started out with my tremendous Lover I had yet to learn that love is not so much receiving as giving, not so much possessing as being possessed. (Isn't it Bishop Sheen who tells us this?) I *did* know that love is rooted in the will and not in the emotions. I had no illusions when I entered on my role as bride of Christ. Now, looking backward, I can say that in the ups and downs of religious life, in the sorrows inseparable from *any* life, it has been the conscious dignity of this role that has supported me. I had leaned on the strong arm of One who is tender, wise, and loving. He has never failed me. Failures there have been on my side, but I have found Him quick to forgive. The passing of the years has made no difference except to tighten the bonds between us. Love does not age.

The wonderful thing about all this is its reality. It is not an attitude, not a pious fancy, not a state of mind, but an overwhelming truth. In a wider sense, every soul in grace wears a wedding garment. Every Christian can refer to Jesus as the Bridegroom of his soul. In fact, the sacrament of marriage is a type of the soul's union with God. But for a religious, this relationship is unique. The virgin soul who renounces earthly marriage to give herself by vow to Christ enters on a new and special kind of union with Him, a union which is everlasting. She begins in time what she will continue in eternity.

This is why the death of a sister is no occasion for tears. Long ago she knelt at the altar and chose Jesus for her portion. She promised to admit no other lover. But she never saw Him. She lived by faith. Now death bends over to lift the veil of separation and bring the lovers face to face. This is the *perfect* wedding day. At such time I hug my secret as I did the day that Sister Patricia gave me the first inkling of it, many years ago.

Sometimes these nuns are old, and disease has done its worst to them. To those on the outside it looks as if a very weak and tired old person is entering on the coasts of peace and rest. But to us on the inside the air is bright with wedding bells. We know that after a long night of waiting the day is at hand. "Behold the Bridegroom cometh, go ye forth to meet Him." Lovely, isn't it? To enjoy an everlasting marriage feast, for which you have been rehearsing all your life.

And so my vocation was touched off by a wedding. I became a nun because I wanted to love and to be loved. With both experiences my cup has brimmed. In loving God I have loved countless others who crossed my path as pupils, converts, or friends. They have added priceless things to my life. They go on enriching me, for love's cycle is unending.

Some there are who would say that at sixteen I was too young to know the true meaning of love; but they, not I, have missed the boat. And if *you* do not believe that a girl of sixteen is capable of great love, human and divine, ask our Blessed Lady. Only a little maiden, she was already deep in love with St. Joseph when she was wounded by a white shaft of the burning love of the Holy Spirit. Her surrender to the divine predilection echoes in these words: "Behold the handmaid of the Lord; be it done unto me according to thy word." For her, too, Annunciation day was bridal day.

VIOLETS ARE FRAGRANT

SISTER MARY PHILIP, C.S.C.[1]

"My Darling Daughter,

NEAR the shore the brown water laps gently through the reeds and the bulrushes, and now and again a startled pelican rises with a mournful cry and a great flapping of wings. If you were here, we should be out fishing on the edge of one of the sandbars, or maybe over on the wing dam, and I suppose I ought to be over there now myself. For over here it is too lonely — since you have gone.

"Your letter came just as I was leaving the office, but I can't bring myself to read it yet. Even getting it is a bittersweet pleasure, a strange mingling of anguish and joy. When you first left, I tore each letter open eagerly, positive that that would be the one which would tell me that you weren't made to be a nun, and that you were coming back home. But now that you've taken your vows, that hope is gone forever. But I'm still not satisfied. Why? I keep asking myself. Why? Why such an austere life as that in one of the active orders of the Church? Sure, I know that a judge ought to know all the answers. And

---

[1] *Sister Mary Philip was born in Dubuque, Iowa. On completing her high school course she joined the Congregation of the Sisters of Holy Cross, whose mother house is at Notre Dame, Indiana. In addition to teaching and nursing, this community does missionary work in several foreign countries. Sister Philip is on the faculty of the Academy of St. Teresa, Boise, Idaho.*

I do know most of them. In fact, I can give them as easily as does your mother to those who still ask if you are really happy. Vocation is an easy word to say — but a hard one to understand. Maybe your mother understands the meanings. I am frank to admit that I don't. Maybe —"

The man paused. Even though the top of the convertible was rolled back, the humidity was oppressive. The clouds were gathering for another thunderstorm. He'd better get going, he thought, and slipped both pen and paper back into the pocket of his coat. Besides, he admitted to himself, that was no kind of letter to send to anyone, much less to his own daughter. He knew that. But there was just a slim chance that if he could once get it all down on paper in an orderly fashion, something like a brief, maybe then he would understand it himself. At least understand it a bit more than he did now.

If only she were here with him, it would be easy. He could see her now, as she was a few short years ago, in the tangle of bleeding hearts and lilies of the valley and columbine that she called a garden, in the tangle of color and sunshine and fragrance that made the day so glorious. Just being alive was wonderful. You could tell that from the intent way she viewed the universe from the cool green terrace on which she was lying. There were grass stains on her knees and elbows, and some on her dress. And cool green prickles of grass against her neck and arms.

He watched her, as through half-closed eyes she followed a cloud-dragon in the pursuit and capture of a snowy lamb — or was it a white cat? She couldn't be sure. She yawned. Summer afternoons always made her sleepy. The dragon himself had completely disappeared now, and some more lambs were skipping across the blue field of the sky. She yawned again, then turned and smiled at him in sudden surprise.

The only sounds were sleepy sounds. In the distance the calliope on the big white river packet, *Mississippi Lady,* heralded its return from an all-day excursion up the river. It was a lonesome sound, though the tune was jazz. And it always started an inner loneliness that hurt more than a headache or a toothache. Well, life was like that, he mused. Only you couldn't let it get you down. He reached for the letter again — the one he had just started; he glanced through it, and then crumpled it in his strong brown hands. What was the use of dodging? What was the use of hedging? What he really wanted to say to her was: "Why did you become a nun? Why you?"

For anyone else, sure, the life was fine. Sisters were good people. The world needed them. But why his girl? Why not, say, Emmy Lou, who lived next door? There was a nice, quiet girl — not a cyclone, like someone else he knew. Emmy Lou was pious, he supposed. She never did much of anything, of course, unlike someone he knew who lighted just long enough to eat and sleep.

There was nothing, to be sure, to keep him from asking the question that troubled him. But it was such a blunt one. Besides, he always had a strong conviction that his love for her should include unquestioning trust in her following of whatever star. And if the star didn't lead him — if, in fact, he couldn't even see its light — that was just his hard luck. Only she was a part of him, and that part was seeing and following something which he should be understanding and sharing, while he was still wrestling with the single word: *Why?*

Why? Well, maybe some day he'd find out. Maybe some day like this one, some letter like the one which was still in his pocket, some letter like the one he was still so reluctant to open because he had not yet been able to steel himself against the loss of her — her laughter, her swift and unexpected bursts of anger with her equally swift tenderness to make amends — maybe some day such a letter would hold the answer in some word or line. Maybe . . . his fingers reached out for the white envelope with her writing. Eagerly he drew it from his inner pocket and ripped it open. The letter was a thick one, and the writing was small. He glanced at the sky. The storm was moving down the river, and patches of blue were showing in the spaces left by the sullen gray clouds that rolled off heavily and reluctantly. He glanced back at the letter which trembled ever so slightly in his hands. Just for an instant he closed his eyes. "Let this be it!" he prayed. "Let this be it!" Then he turned back to the stiff white pages.

"Dearest Daddy,

"This letter is one I've been wanting to write you for ever so long, and I'm going to start out by asking you to forget that it's a letter. I was going to say that you should close your eyes and pretend we're out fishing together — not over on the sand-bar, though, for that's pretty hot on days like these. Let's stay over on the shore, over where it's cool and shady, and the willows lean over to look at their long shadows in the water. The fishing's not too good because of last night's rain, so let's just talk instead.

"Neither one of us could ever hide anything from the other, and though you've been wonderful about my leaving home and becoming a nun, I have been increasingly aware of a definite barrier between us. You've never put it in so many words. But it's in every letter you write — between the lines, of course. I know you don't doubt my vocation. But I have the feeling sometimes that, even unknowingly, you are fighting against it. Probably tearing the word 'Why?' to shreds fifty times a day. Perhaps even wondering if the vocation wasn't meant for Emmy Lou, and went to the wrong house instead.

"It would be so very easy, and it would simplify things for everyone, if I could just say, 'Daddy, darling, here is a nice volume of the *Lives of the Saints* where, on page 234, you will find the story of my vocation, and that of every other girl who has left her home and everyone she holds dear, to follow and to bind herself by triple vow to a Lover she can't even show the family.' But I can't do that. For just as every love story is a unique and personal experience, so is that of every vocation.

"And both have much in common. For in both, the focus of

life is not on self, but rather on the will of the Beloved. In a religious vocation Christ calls, and the soul answers. But between the call and the answer sometimes many years elapse. And sometimes the soul is afraid to listen. And sometimes the soul refuses to say 'Yes.'

"But sometimes the answer is a spontaneous yes, for the soul has really and truly and literally fallen in love with Christ, and knows with certainty that only in Him, through Him, and by Him will she achieve happiness both here and hereafter.

"I often wonder myself when first I thought of being a nun. I don't know. I do remember, though, so very vividly, the very first time I saw the Sisters of the Holy Cross. I thought I had never in my life seen anything so beautiful as the Breton peasant costume which constitutes the habit of the order. The Breton costume with its white starched, fluted cap; the white, heart-shaped collar; the military black cape and skirt; the bright blue cord; the silver heart; and the large rosary to remind one of our Lady.

"Through the graciousness of these sisters to whom I went to school, I learned the graciousness of Christ, a Christ who was my Changeless Friend and who loved me deeply and personally. Through the dedication of these sisters to the education of youth, as well as to the care of hospital and mission work at home and on foreign shores — through this dedication made by the perpetual vows of poverty, chastity, and obedience — I saw, from the angle of youth, just what these sisters accomplished for my classmates and my friends.

"For some of the girls, the sisters were the only real mothers they had ever known. For others, they were counselors. For still others, they were friends. For all, they were the fulfillment of a vital and a sacred need. And the love and the help the sisters offered were absolutely selfless. The flowers they received now and then as a token of gratitude or a feast day gift were placed on the altar where a loving Christ waited to comfort and to advise, or in the Lady Chapel where we poured out our confidences before her who is our life, our sweetness, and our hope.

"But still none of this is the answer to the question, Why? Why you? Why not someone else? Why now? Why not one, or two, or five, or ten years from now? Of course, every girl has her plans and her dreams. They follow the pattern of life as she sees it. And the pattern unfailingly includes wealth, and love, and happiness, and even sometimes fame. It never includes want, or privation, or suffering, or loneliness in any of their various guises.

"But then, suddenly and strangely, the pattern is in shreds and tossed aside, a worthless thing. For the dream of wealth and love and comfort has become instead the cry of the hungry, the needy, the forsaken — and from their eyes looks out the Christ who said that He counts as done to Himself whatever is done to the least of His brethren.

"So it was with me. He who had thrown St. Paul from his horse, only turned and looked at me. But what had I to do with the least of His brethren? It was all just my imagination, I told myself. And even if it weren't, I couldn't measure up. I just couldn't. I wasn't unselfish. I wasn't heroic. I needed no great insight to come to those conclusions. That was the score. Therefore, wasn't it gross presumption even to think of following? What if all this were just an illusion? An illusion which would fade when I started to follow it, and would, in consequence, leave me cynical and bitter.

"And worse still, what if it were not an illusion? Once I started following such a Leader, there could be no turning back from the way that led to a hill called Calvary. I could think of twenty arguments against being a nun to every one argument for being one. But the glance of Christ remained steadfast, penetrating the pitiful excuses I advanced for refusing to follow Him. And then, suddenly, it was over — this extended game of hide-and-seek which I had been playing. There were no more places to hide. He had won. And suddenly the world was transformed. It was a radiant world, a glorious world, for I had fallen in love. The impact was so sudden and so overwhelming as to admit of no doubt. Christ loved me. He wanted me. There was only one way for me to say yes to God, and that was to be a nun.

"Even as an old lady of a hundred and ten I shall remember the day I received the letter from the Mistress of Novices telling me that I had been accepted. The thermometer outside registered fifteen degrees below zero, and with the letter still in my hand, I raced down the street to follow a clanging fire engine. Mother was awaiting me on my return, and none of my explanations could convince her that I wasn't on the verge of pneumonia, or at least that I had escaped frost bite. Why, I wasn't even cold. On the crest of joy, there is no need for thermometers.

"But there were other days also. There was the morning I awoke with something heavy pressing on my heart. Then, I remembered. This was the day I was leaving. And nothing would ever be the same again. Nothing. The drabness of the February morning peered in through my window, and pressed against the grimy, soot-streaked windows of the dingy station. Nothing would ever be the same again.

" 'Train's on time,' the ticket agent wheezed as he put the money in the cash drawer, and slid my ticket in its gay envelope across the counter. You took it, and gave my hand a tight little squeeze as we went out together into the winter morning. Remember? Remember, too, the corsage of violets that you and Mother gave me there on the squalid platform in the dismal February dawn? It was a promise of springtime, and the remembrance of all the laughter and love we had had together. And now that time was almost gone. A glaring headlight pierced the grayness of the morning as you pinned the violets on my fur jacket. They were very sweet, and very blue, and I could feel their softness against my throat.

" 'Wait!' I wanted to say. 'Wait! I'm not going after all. I've changed my mind. I'm not leaving any of you — ever!' "

"But with a clang of bells and hiss of steam the train drew

up to a stop. And I knew I was going. My face felt stiff and unnatural, as though a smile had been carved in wood which was stiff and unyielding.

" 'Board!' called the conductor. 'Board!'

"We said good-by again, and I stepped onto the train. Laughing, I turned and waved, but on my lips was the taste of tears. Like someone moving in a nightmare, I was on my way. Where my heart had been, now there was only an aching stone. Some girls meet the hurdle of bitter opposition. Others meet the hurdle of love. That one I had met, and knew its power to shatter.

"I watched the familiar landscape, now somehow strange and unfamiliar, in the half-light of the February dawn — the ice-bound streams; the stark, bare trees; the river, desolate and still. I tried to keep from remembering the summer, when there were pond lilies of gold and white and pink instead of barren patches of snow. I couldn't let myself think beyond that — to the fishing we had together, to the picnics, to anything that brought back anyone I loved. I just wasn't brave enough.

"The little farmhouses along the way looked cozy and warm and bright. And so did the wayside stations with their clusters of passengers waiting to board the train. But I was a stranger now. A wayfarer. The order I was entering had houses from coast to coast. I could be sent anywhere. Any time. The obedience was military. Dimly I recalled something about the Son of Man having no place to lay His head. Nothing would ever be the same again, for I was a bride going to meet my Beloved at the trysting place where He was awaiting me.

"And then, suddenly, I was here with Him, and all was well. Dedicated to our Lady, the members of the order diffuse the love that is from her, the Mother of Fair Love, with whom I had fallen in love one spring twilight when I left before her worn and battered shrine a little bunch of flowers that held my heart. Now I knew I had been right. For in the Holy Rule of the order I had joined are the words:

'The chief aim of the Sisters of the Holy Cross is to study the glorious Standard after which the Congregation is named, and to become living copies of the Divine Mother who stood by it on Calvary.'

"Perhaps love for that same Mother had been the mysterious attraction which had drawn me to the Sisters of the Holy Cross at Notre Dame, Indiana. Or perhaps that love had been for many years in the process of formation, and each Sign of the Cross contributed further to its growth. I knew now that I was where I belonged, where God wanted me to be. And now I know what I didn't know then — that the yes of generous young girls can mean the ultimate opening of another school, and that their refusal to enter religious life can mean that countless children are kept from the knowledge and the love of Christ.

"And the monotony of the religious life? That is one factor which simply does not exist. Actually, it's fun to be a nun — and I dare anyone who really knows to say it isn't. Just as an example, our Congregation has establishments from Massachusetts to California, from Michigan to Texas, over the Atlantic Ocean to South America and East Pakistan. This year I may be teaching girls who are more at home on horseback than anywhere else, girls who ride in rodeos, rope cattle, and are crack marksmen with a rifle. Next year I may be teaching the daughters of diplomats in Washington, D. C. The business of the day is not confined alone to teaching. It may, and frequently does, include waiting on table, doing dishes, gardening, counseling, lecturing, writing, painting, cooking. And all of it is a prayer hallowed, from the first Sign of the Cross in the morning to the last Sign of the Cross in the evening, by the reminder of St. Paul: Whether you eat or drink or whatever else you do, do it all for the honor and glory of God.

"But this letter is becoming bulkier by the minute. In fact, if I don't stop soon, I may have to send it parcel post. And with it all, I don't know that I've answered your question *Why*.

Quite honestly, I don't know that I ever could except with the single word *love*. I think perhaps our Lady will have to answer it, as only she can — by filling your heart with a share of that same love and the deep peace which she has given to

Your darling daughter."

A cool breeze from the river stirred the letter even as he tried to fold it, and a shaft of sudden sunlight glanced over his shoulder. Somehow everything was right and as it should be. And it all made sense, even to a judge. He smiled as he started the car. Tomorrow was another day.

HAPPILY EVER AFTER

SISTER ST. GEORGE, C.S.J.[1]

I SAT down on a chair with my feet stretched out in front of me and raised a scratchy abundance of skirt to my knees. I laughed out loud. One foot was in strange contrast to the rest of my postulant's dress. Beside the cotton stocking and the sturdy oxford on my right foot were the sheer nylon and the fancy pump still on my left. "Well, one has to come off," I grinned, "and so it's farewell to nylons."

That September afternoon I said farewell to more than nylons. In fact, it seemed that I had said farewell to a whole world, a whole life — Mom and the family, Towser and the crowd — everything that meant seventeen.

How did it happen that I came to be here? How had I managed to exchange the stylish items hanging in my closet for the long skirts, stiff collar, and black veil that were only a prelude to a life in more starch and yardage? I suppose the question has the same meaning as another one that I can remember hearing for an age or two and that still comes up

---

[1] *Sister St. George is a member of the Congregation of the Sisters of St. Joseph of Carondelet and is at present a teacher at Mount St. Mary's College, 12001 Chalon Road, Los Angeles, California. The works of this community include teaching, nursing, and other charitable activities. The Western Province, to which Sister St. George belongs, has its headquarters at the House of Studies, 11999 Chalon Road, Los Angeles, California.*

every now and then. It presents itself in a hundred different ways.

My fourth grade chums and I are at our lunch-time game of jacks. Over the intricacies of my down-pats I cut in on Mary Ellen's rhapsodies over the kind of house and the number of children she will have when she grows up, with the definite, "I'm going to be a sister."

"Gee! What do you want to be a sister for?"

My best friend's mother remarks: "I hear Eva wants to go to the convent. Why does she want to do that?"

My father glares down at freshman me. "You! in the convent! What in heaven's name do you want to be a nun for?"

A chalk-dusty afternoon in my classroom brings a little girl to my desk with a pensive, "Sister, why did you become a sister?"

I kneel at my prie-dieu and turn the pages of my *Following* to see: "Consider often why thou hast come here."

Now that I think about it, the answer is simple. Perhaps it may sound selfish, but it's theologically correct. I wanted to be happy. I knew positively that the sisters were happy — happier than any other people I met. Therefore . . .

I suppose, though, that I should explain my reason a little more before everyone decides to go to the convent or else decides that I must have a warped personality in looking for happiness first in a convent.

Of course, God never intended everyone to be *a religious*, although everyone has the obligation to be *religious*. He did intend that all His creatures be happy — that's why He made us, you and me. Some people are more easily satisfied than others. However, I wasn't too old before I began to realize that the thrill of a new doll didn't last very long, that a new dress didn't stay new, that class honors were here for today only, that corsages wilted, that convertibles broke down.

Apparently, things weren't going to make me everlastingly happy. Would persons do it? Well, my parents, my brothers and sisters, my best chums, the boys I knew were all right, but there were many times when they didn't fit in. They couldn't see or know so many of the things bottled up inside me, and I couldn't tell them. And so I had to look for my happiness with *the Person*.

Not being the frilly type of miss, I didn't make my decision under the influence of soft music, teary swoons, or any of that emotional froth. I knew very little about the religious life. I had heard about something called meditation, and I knew that the rule called for rising at the ungodly hour of five. A vague notion about Monday's being consecrated to doing the community laundry floated around somewhere in my mind.

You might think it was stupid of me to act on so little knowledge, but though I seem to have been hazy on particulars, my principles were clear enough. They had to be if they were going to stand up under the barrage sponsored by everyone in creation who got wind of my plans.

I made a small-scale inventory and found that I could probably have managed, as other people do, if I had chosen to follow a profession in the world. Eventually, I might have married and added a fairly respectable family to the sum total of society. I could have saved my soul and, after a fashion, I could have been reasonably happy to boot. My mother was great for dragging out this argument.

My father used to work on a different angle. I liked nice things, my own things, and — he used to underline this — I liked my own way. How was I going to fit vows of poverty and obedience into that setup?

My friends dug up the traditional line — being buried in a convent, ugh! — those uncomfortable habits — no fun — and so on. Even if I had wanted to close my eyes to the con's, I couldn't have. My pro's really had to hold water.

To my mother I showed that the opportunity of educating a few of my own children — who would probably grow up to be as spoiled as my nephews and nieces anyhow — couldn't compare with the chance of teaching hundreds and raising a really sizable family — for God. I tried to show my father that liking nice things, my own things, and still giving them up was my down payment on an exceptionally good buy. As for having my own way, wasn't that a form of the urge for freedom? Wouldn't the religious life give me a better and a greater freedom? Traveling light gets you where you're going, don't you know.

I canned the cloister walls business rather effectively by mentioning that if all such bosh were true, convents would be empty. Since they weren't, and since sisters were human beings, happy ones, mind you, I didn't think their homes were first cousins to a female edition of Alcatraz.

In sophomore year I took my first official step. I spoke to my pastor about entering. Did I say *spoke* to him? I mean that after swallowing my heart a few times and coaxing my pulse down to a reasonable rate of speed, I managed to walk into the awful presence and state my business.

My pastor, being a man of wisdom and experience and, under normal conditions, one of my best friends, promptly produced the cold water apparatus for dispelling false notions about vocations. He trotted out the customary interrogatives, erected some superlative hurdles, and left me feeling very much like the loser in a bout with the Devil's Advocate. Nevertheless, he didn't say no, but only, "All right — but not until after graduation." That was that.

Of all the things that passed in that interview, I remembered one especially. To the pastor's terse, "Which community?" I had zipped back, "Our sisters." I wonder now how he knew which sisters I meant since more than one group of them were connected with our school and parish societies. I knew, but what made me so definite?

Spirit is a difficult quality to define, but it's a terrific mover. It moved me — moved me through the little sister fidgeting over the wreath on my First Communion veil, moved me through

the aproned efficiency of the sister directing June cleanup in our
fifth grade classroom, moved me through the matter-of-fact
goodness which each sister I met had tucked into her make-up
as basic equipment.

Later, with pages torn from calendars and the end of senior
year signaling time for final decision, I appreciated that spirit
still more. These sisters weren't self-constituted traffic directors
on a one-way road labeled "convent." Those who knew my plans
didn't mention them unless I spoke first. More from their attitude in this matter than in any other way, I learned that my
vocation, or anyone's vocation for that matter, is something
special, something between God and the lucky person He has
chosen. The sisters loved their vocation; they respected mine.
Thanks be to God!

The day set for my entrance into the postulate was — don't
laugh — Labor Day. At the time, parting from the family wasn't
much of a wrench because everyone was convinced that I
would be back home shortly. Mom worried about the wisdom of
buying a one-way ticket; a round-trip seemed much more advisable. "See ya in a week," was my little brother's affectionate
last word.

He didn't see me in a week — or two weeks or even three.
By that time I was wrapped up in the do's and don'ts of a bell-
regulated life. When Christmas came, and my trunk did not
appear on their front porch, the family planned a sort of rescue
expedition. I think their pride needed a band-aid when they
found that I was perfectly content. Definitely, I wasn't coming
home.

Somehow the six months of my postulancy whizzed by
leaving me with pinpricked fingers and one handmade habit —
my first. What fun my companions and I had in that time,
especially as we prepared for our reception with the fitting of
white dresses, learning to walk in fancy shoes for the last time,
speculating on our new names, and then — retreat!

St. Joseph's Day came. The ceremony of reception, my being

clothed with the habit, meeting my family afterward, getting used to the name that was now mine for keeps — these were the beginnings of that new part of my life: those wonderful, never-a-dull-moment years of my novitiate.

But, like the time of postulancy, so my period of novitiate melted into yesterdays. After counting days and weeks and months for so long, after watching each group of senior novices kneel at the altar to receive the badge of their profession, my turn came too. My hand closed around the precious treasure that is my profession crucifix.

My three and a half years of temporary vows were filled with the work of the classroom and the manual labor of the convent. This was the time for proving the theory of the novitiate with practice under fire.

Again it was my turn to pronounce my vows, but this time it was forever. Believe me, "forever" is a wonderful word when it means that God and your community and you are all agreed to belong to one another, world without end.

Sometimes perspective does a great deal toward improving a view. I see now that my desire for happiness was not the single motive force which brought me to enter the convent. My desire had a companion — conviction, the conviction that God wanted me. Remember, I didn't say a sentimental feeling, or even a feeling. I said a *conviction*, one of those realities like two and two are four. Try getting sentimental about that.

Both desire and conviction were and are necessary to see me safely over the rough spots in the road, and there are rough spots. Religious life is not jolt-free, but religious life does provide the backbone to stand the jolts and the funnybone to tape up the bruises.

It's definitely old hat now to talk about that tremendous attribute called womanliness. The great feminine trend at present is to contrive to become a girl grown old without ever having looked in on or attempted to imitate the valiant woman of the Scriptures, who put her hand to strong things. Yet of all the blessings that have come to me with my vocation, I think that the companionship of the good women, the strong women who are my sisters, rates four stars.

I like to apply to my vocation what the Old Testament applies to Wisdom, "All good things come to me together with her." These good things don't figure in our world of dollars and cents. They are rather intangible — things like the glory of midnight Mass at Christmas, the joy of seeing the long line of novices stretching out to support the truth of my choice, the confidence of little children in Sister.

I don't worry that these good things will not serve in barter as coin of the realm. I'm saving them all up for my one-way trip to the place where all of us, please God, will live happily ever after.

SO GLAD I PLUNGED IN DEEP

SISTER M. PETER JOHN, O.S.F.[1]

POOR Mother! She tried so hard to make a nice little girl of me. Probably her worst trial was the time I was literally dragged home, soaking wet, defiant, crying, shivering, still insisting that I didn't mind a wet swimming suit under my coveralls, and that "I *always* went around like that." After all, I was a very mature nine-and-a-half-almost-ten, and I had done a wonderful thing in spite of my earache. I had managed to do some sort of dive from the high board with Dinny. The fact that the high board was enough to alarm even "great big" boys pleased me immensely; but the fact that Dinny broke his leg on this last attempt was enough to depress even a nine-and-a-half-almost-ten-year-old. My earache got worse, my mother grew more concerned by the moment, and my father began getting me ready for the hospital. Dinny was the one that was hurt, not me. Unless you count the earache, that is.

No, I really hadn't meant to disobey my mother. It just happened that way. Dinny said he had a new trick. So, when

---

[1] Sister M. Peter John, a native of Fort Dodge, Iowa, became a Catholic during her student days at Iowa State University and five months after her baptism she entered the Third Order of St. Francis. This community has its headquarters at St. Francis of Assisi Convent, 3221 South Lake Drive, Milwaukee 7, Wisconsin. During the past year Sister Peter John has been studying art at Cardinal Stritch College in Milwaukee.

he got off guard duty, we just naturally tried it. He was very old in my estimation — at least nineteen — and although he had a few moments of idiocy when the older girls came around, I loved him and put up with these disturbing periods very loyally. On this particular day I had been forbidden to go in swimming because of my bad ear. It had been lanced a week previously and was just a *little* sore, nothing serious, I thought. But when Dinny suggested the new trick, the fish in me responded before I thought, and that was when it happened! The next moment was the beginning of my search for God, the beginning of my desire to possess Him totally, the beginning of my life.

Dinny was explaining to me the way I should jump off his back as soon as we got a third of the way down. I was in my usual place on top of his shoulders. He began to spring, slowly at first, then increasing in speed and height. I never looked down during this warming up process because I was too frightened, though I would rather die than acknowledge that fact. Instead, I looked straight out in front of me; and this day I prayed even harder than usual. Then the terrible remembrance of my mother's orders — "Darling, not today; no, you mayn't go in today" — came upon me.

"Dear God," I prayed, "I just remembered. I'm not supposed to go in. Dear God, don't let anything happen to me; don't let Dinny make a mistake. And God, please come from behind the cloud; and God, please fix everything forever."

Somehow, I always thought of God as being in clouds, or behind them. As I prayed, I knew that God actually was there with Dinny and me. I always loved God, but somehow I felt extra close that moment. I still remember the impression vividly. God would always fix everything. I need never worry.

It happened in a split second. I came up all right; then I looked for Dinny's blond head to bob up too. I couldn't find him. People were gathered at the corner of the pool by the small boards, and of course those silly girls were there. I knew something had happened, something bad. Mr. Jackson made a big fuss over me and felt all my bones to see if they were broken. He said he felt responsible because he managed the pool. He kept mumbling things I didn't understand, things about fate, I think. My ear began to pound fiercely. I didn't even get to talk with Dinny before the men took him away. Right then and there I told God a few things which nice little Baptist girls who go to Sunday School and sing sweet little songs didn't ordinarily say to God. I remember sobbing bitterly and looking at that same cloud, saying "Dear God, I sure don't like You any more at all. I'll never love You again unless You're a little nicer. I'm finished, dear God; it's the end. So there!" I concluded with some words my father used to say on certain occasions — words which made my mother frown and utter reproaches to the effect that such things should not be said in front of little girls.

I am firmly convinced that this earliest impression of God's closeness, my reliance on Him, and then the accident were providential means to bring me face to face with His love and protection in years to come.

The result of the swimming episode was the answer to my childish prayer. God really did become a little "nicer." In fact, He brought me in contact with the first Catholics I had ever known. These were the good sisters in the hospital. My father was on the staff of Mercy Hospital, and naturally I went there when it became evident that my ear was not to be trifled with. In spite of my efforts to conceal the pain, my left ear was protruding far enough to make even me gasp in astonishment. As soon as I knew I was to be operated on, I suddenly lost all feeling of discomfort. A doctor's daughter often has ample opportunity to peer into surgical volumes, and I associated operations will all sorts of steel instruments, saws, and needles. My favorite volume of Daddy's was *Surgical Techniques in Amputations,* or some such title. This positively intrigued me. However, now that I imagined I would be the victim, I was absolutely horror-stricken! I had visions of my ear coming off, in surgically correct slices, in spite of my father's explanations of all the latest techniques. Soon, however, it was over, and a new adventure was beginning for me — an adventure which continued for seven years — and more. I involved myself in the intrigues of the Catholic Church.

The sisters gave me a lovely little dewdrop, which later was lost in a grand fight with one of my friends. Had I not treasured my dewdrop so much, the loss wouldn't have been felt so keenly. Had Mickey not taken my flint marble, I would not have hit him, and had I not sat on him and pulled his hair, he would not have pulled the little chain with the precious medal off my neck.

Poor Mother! She tried so hard to make a nice little girl out of me. Daddy said I would grow out of my boyish tastes, but I know Mother must have had her doubts. Daddy and I must have cost her many hours of heroic endurance, yet she patiently encouraged most of our brainstorms. Like the time Daddy very suddenly decided we would take a vacation up north in the wilderness without any planning at all. He saw an article in *The National Geographic* about the Canadian wilds and decided that, since he had no babies to deliver at the time, he could get away. He came home from the office with a new Johnson motor for his boat, reservations for a guide, and a new grease job on his car. He brought me a real fly rod and, best of all, an honest-to-goodness pair of boy's ranger boots. That was when I heard Mother say with a sigh, "Honestly, dear, how do you expect her to act like a girl? If you would just help a little." With that, I promptly resumed my table-setting chore, reflecting that as long as I was doomed to be a girl, I still had plenty of time later on to act like one.

It was during this period that I forgot for a short time the impression made upon me by the sisters and that little Miraculous Medal called a dewdrop. The vacation up north was the occasion of great grace, however, for it was there that I learned the Hail Mary.

Dad taught me how to cast a fly and play a black bass on the end of my line, how to pick a turtle off a log with a .22 rifle, and how to repair an outboard motor. I used to watch him often in the summer, but now I was trusted with the boat and my own special fly rod. On rainy days — and it rained most of the time — Mother would indulge in her favorite pastime: reading aloud to me. We were on *As You Like It* and though, when the Shakespearean process first started I balked, I had come to love it. Mother would explain it to me so that I could assimilate it somewhat, and soon I began comparing almost everything to a stage and the seven parts. My father would listen attentively and, between exits and entrances, tell me what a wonderful mother I had. I would nod approval vehemently, though I didn't realize then just how wonderful she really was. Often he kissed her on the forehead; sometimes they would dance to the tune of music on the radio. We were a very happy three-some — Mother, Daddy, and I.

Then one evening the telephone rang. Daddy was called into the Army, and he had to report in a week to Livingston, Louisiana. It was decided that Mother would go with him to make arrangements, and in the meantime I was to stay on with the resort owners until Mother called for me. It was all very exciting; and since it would mean a new place to live and a new school in the fall, I was thrilled. I would be living down south. War is a terrible thing, but the vastness of it and its atrocities do not stir one as much as when it is felt immediately. My father wasn't overseas yet, and so, for a time at least, he was safe. If Mother was worried, she didn't show it; of course, she never let me down anyway.

The resort owners were good Catholics. Each night they said the rosary together; each Sunday they went by boat across the lake to Mass. Soon I began going along. I learned the Hail

Mary, did not eat meat on Friday, and knew how to go to confession. This last piece of information I obtained from a prayer book which was just "lying around." From then on, for a period of two or three weeks, I would confess to God all my transgressions according to the little black book I had appropriated. When Louise, the resort owner's daughter, tried to find it, I told her I just couldn't imagine what had happened to it! In each confession I added . . . "and I stole this book, God." These confessions had such an effect on me that I even made an effort to become more ladylike. Of course, I never succeeded completely, but I did return the black book.

The new school in Alexandria, Louisiana, was a wonderful experience for me. Here I really began to grow up. But then my father was transferred to Texas. Because this happened in the middle of the school year, Mother deemed it wise for me to continue my schooling in Alexandria while she went with Dad. To broaden my education, as my father put it, I was to have as temporary guardians a kosher Jewish family. They were Army people, a lieutenant and his wife. I began to feel the loneliness for something which I didn't understand. That something was God.

An Army town is a fascinating place, especially for a fourteen-year-old-girl. I had an allowance, a great deal of freedom, and an insatiable curiosity for anything savoring of adventure. I had always been taught that to go around with boys, to enter drugstores and read comic books, to write silly notes, to accept wild rides in hopped-up cars, and to moon over movie stars were quite beneath my dignity. Mother always said my time would come. Any friends I had were always welcome in our home and made a part of the family. But in Alexandria social customs seemed to be different. My friends would tell me how easy it was to pick up an attractive soldier and go to a movie. I did not act on their suggestions, however, and if Alexandria did nothing else for me, it brought me the realization that I was becoming a young lady after all, at least in some respects.

It was simply God's Providence watching over me, though I didn't know it at the time.

The next school year I spent in Texas; from there we moved to California. Dad was sent overseas. It was in the Pasadena Opera House that I began to want the Church.

It was a warm spring evening. Mother and I were walking hurriedly to be on time for *La Bohème*. Since I ushered, I had to be there early. Each time we went to a performance, a little of the excitement clung to me for weeks. *La Bohème* is a sad opera, and Mother wasn't at all impressed. She said that Mimi's dying aria sounded like "One Meat Ball," one of the popular songs of that time. I was very much touched by it, on the other hand, and I thought her comment very . . . well, just *very!*

On the way home the thought of death played on my mind. We used to walk home on nice evenings, and this was a nice evening. It took me fourteen blocks to remember that Hail Mary and how it ended. I knew it had something about death in it, and I liked that concept of death. I felt much better to think that maybe Mary prayed for people like Mimi. From the moment that the Hail Mary came back to my mind, I repeated it often during the days that followed.

Graduation from high school held no great interest for me, for my heart was already in college. The morning after I received my diploma Mother and I left for Iowa State, where I was to take a pre-med course, starting with the summer quarter.

There I was destined to be baptized and to find my desire to become a sister and to belong totally to Christ. It was the era of plaid shirts (shirt tails out), jeans, saddle shoes, and unobtainable cigarettes. These last didn't concern me too much, except that once I was so surprised to find a store selling some off-name brand by the carton that I invested in two of them — two whole cartons. Lounging very sophisticatedly in my red shirt, jeans, and horn-rimmed glasses, I disconcertedly tried, between unskilled puffs of my new investment, to learn the life processes of *amoeba proteus*. Disgusted with the whole business — I knew I was not acting in accord with my home training — I promptly changed clothes, gave the cigarettes away, scrubbed my room, aired it out, and resumed a more dignified, if more simple, existence.

Religion was often discussed among the girls on our floor of the dormitory. My roommate was a Mormon, but she didn't practice her religion. The two girls down the hall were Catholics but . . . ! The girls in the room opposite mine were Methodists, and our house mother was an Episcopalian. And I? I simply *was*. I called myself a Christian but of no denomination. My religion consisted in talking to God now and then, going to church infrequently, and roundly denouncing my Catholic friends for staying Catholic since they didn't go to Mass. They should be either *good* Catholics or none at all, in my estimation. My impression of the Catholic Church was that it was a grotesque red specter of formidable proportions which enveloped one so completely that one could never escape. I respected it and loved the Hail Mary; but as far as investigating its doctrine was concerned, I felt that once I did I would be compelled to believe — not forced to enter the Church, but compelled to subject my poor weak will to the discipline of centuries. I certainly didn't want that! But it happened!

There was a priest on the campus who took care of the Newman Club and who was also a very good buddy to the Navy V-12 Unit on the campus. One day, after an inspiring lecture on the evolutionary tendencies of man, a group of us wandered over to the Student Union for cokes. The boys were quite excited and thrilled with the idea of man's development and what was to come. I considered it very intellectual and also very empty. Then I met Father Joe. Some of the Vets knew him and introduced me. When they brought up the subject of evolution, the priest explained the Church's stand and the infusion of the human soul. That I liked. It was reasonable. So I grabbed at Truth. I found it refreshing, strong, and challenging. Grace always is.

From then on I read everything about Catholicism I could get my hands on. I even started by robbing the vestibule of St. Cecilia's Church of *Our Sunday Visitor, Why* pamphlets, and other reading matter. These I didn't pay for, because I would never be caught giving anything to that reddish-brown specter. Still, I could not resist it. It began to lose its terror. I began to want it terribly.

I was baptized after a late afternoon zoology class. I shall never forget that April afternoon. In my suit pocket was carefully tucked a list of all my sins. I tried to memorize it thoroughly and thought I had succeeded. I reviewed it all the time I was trying to find subclavian arteries in pigs. When the time came I forgot everything. Then it was I learned that confession is not a memory job; it's a simple telling process, very much as I used to talk to God about the prayer book I took.

Some of my most precious memories of the road to religion were those early morning walks to St. Cecilia's for Mass and Holy Communion. I could never be grateful enough for my faith. God was neglected by so many, and I wanted to do something about it.

That summer, amid fruit flies and rat cages, I managed to read the lives of many saints. The life of Father William Doyle impressed me greatly, as did the life of St. Francis. I decided that I would be a Franciscan and that I must become one right away. If I had to finish the summer quarter, at least I could begin to live my ideal. I tried . . . and I failed. I all but climbed a pillar like St. Simon Stylites. I was very foolish. But I was a Catholic.

The Imitation of Christ had a profound effect on my life. I *read* it over again and again. Soon my taste for cars and clothes and homecoming dances began to disappear. Christ alone mattered. I didn't see why there weren't more like St. Francis in the world. But, then, I was very immature, and there were a lot of things I didn't see.

June came. My bank account receded. I spent a very sleepless night after I received a letter from the bank telling me that I had overdrawn my account by ninety-two cents. Then I got a job detasseling corn at the wage of fifty cents an hour. My appearance was appalling — red like a parched beet; hands cut from the sharp leaves of the corn. But I was happy, and I was actually earning money.

It was after a hot, wet day in the fields that I betook myself to the chemistry lab to make up an experiment. There, reading over some notes, was a Franciscan nun. Maybe she could tell me how to go about becoming a nun. I had been a Catholic only two months, but that was my ideal. It would be a glorious adventure. It still is and always will be. I learned that Sister was saying her Office. She told me that I should write to the Mother General. That night I did. It was as easy as that.

I might add here that there was no struggle in my case. If there was any struggle at all, it was before I became a Catholic. Sometimes I fought with myself then, but now I saw what I really wanted — to become holy, to glorify Christ, to be one with Him and help save souls. It was a question of gaining something infinitely higher than what I had, something I am at a loss to explain. Once one has seen God's lovableness, everything else is dross.

When the clothes list came, my roommate found it. Then there were parties and gifts. My friends didn't laugh. They might have wondered, but they didn't laugh. The Mother General said I might come in September, though it was unusual to accept converts so soon after baptism. Now, my parents had to be informed, and that was going to be hard.

I tried to explain what I had found, but of course they couldn't understand. Yes, my home was happy, and I had everything to satisfy me. Yes, I liked dances and socials. No, there were no disappointments in my life. If things had been otherwise, people might have seen a reason for my leaving. But I seemed too happy. Finally, Mother gave her consent, saying that I could always come home. Dad reluctantly gave in, too.

Both of them were prompted by very unselfish motives. It wasn't so much the idea of losing me that they minded, for they expected that to happen some day anyway. It was the fear that I was engaging in something that would spell misery and un- happiness for me. They needn't have worried, and they realize that now. They love all my sisters in Christ as they love their own daughter. They are proud to have a nun for a daughter, and I am proud of them too.

So, five months after my baptism, I found myself at the convent door. I had never seen a convent before except from the outside. But I fell in love with my St. Francis Convent as soon as I stepped inside. It was home — God's home and mine!

And that's the story. Happy? Of course! The love of God is like a flame. You can't explain its fire, and you can't tell why it burns so relentlessly in such a one as yourself. It just happens, like falling in love. And why He chose me out of so many is His secret — and mine to thank Him for. It's like the glorious adventure I mentioned before. Each day is filled with new challenges, new opportunities to become like Christ, like St. Francis. A day — what a wonderful creation of God! For a day means time, and time means opportunity — oppor- tunity that sends us soaring, leaping, bounding — higher and higher still — to God.

I'm so glad I plunged in deep!

DANTE AND THE STREETCARS

SISTER KRISTIN, O.S.B.[1]

IF IT hadn't been for Dante and the Pennsylvania Avenue streetcars, this would probably be my thirteenth year at the National Catholic Welfare Conference Bureau of Immigration in Washington, D. C. But six words from Dante had fixed themselves in my mind; and after days tingling with excitement at the office, there were the long rides home on the streetcars. Now the black serge habit the Bishop blessed for me one bright June morning is ten years old and reinforced along the pleats with hundreds of tiny stitches.

I was a junior here at the College of St. Benedict in St. Joseph, Minnesota, when I studied Dante's *Divine Comedy* for the first time. It opened up a new world and a new heaven. My eyes followed St. Bernard's upward pointing to the Light which is God, "light intellectual, full-charged with love, love of true good, full-charged with gladness, gladness which transcendeth every sweetness." Like Dante himself, at the end of

---

[1] *Sister Kristin, a native of Van Hook, North Dakota, became a secretary in the Bureau of Immigration of the National Catholic Welfare Conference, Washington, D. C. Her desire to do God's will finally led her to the Sisters of St. Benedict. Sister Kristin is now an instructor in English at the College of St. Benedict, Saint Joseph, Minnesota, where the mother house of the community is situated. "Dante and the Streetcars" is reprinted from* St. Benedict's Quarterly *by permission of the editors.*

the last canto of the *Paradiso,* "my desire and will were rolled
— even as a wheel that moveth equally — by the love that
moves the sun and the other stars." The bookbinders trimmed
my marginal notes when they put on a new cover last year,
and even though the last letters are gone, I can tell from
the way I wrote at the bottom of page 601, "In His will is
our peace," that I put an exclamation mark after the word.
Those six words lodged in my mind like a tiny stone in an
oyster's shell. And later they brought on as much irritation.
After the Dante course was over, I was sold on doing God's
will.

Sisters have been known to corner likely prospects and suggest
the possibility of a religious vocation. Bent as I was on doing
God's will, attached as I was to St. Benedict's, I believe I would
have transferred to another college if anyone had mentioned
"enter" or "other side" or "nun" to me, as was being done
to one or two of my classmates. I wasn't fighting a vocation.
I had grown up in a tiny town in northwestern North Dakota
where we Catholics were few and where a nun was *not* one
of the things a young girl wanted to be. I just didn't want
spring spoiled by any embarrassing nonsense.

Exactly what God's will might involve became a problem
only when we were college seniors and everyone else in the
class had accepted either a contract or a ring. Much as marriage appealed to me, much as I enjoyed the company of boys,
I knew I didn't really love the fellows who had ring ideas. I
knew I'd enjoy teaching, but I longed to live at home for
a while with my widowed mother, my two brothers and sister,
after hardly seeing them for years. Teaching in the District
of Columbia would require an M.A. we couldn't afford. When
retreat time came, I discovered for the first time that I had
a problem to take to the retreat master.

I'm still thanking God for what Father Godfrey Diekman,
O.S.B., a monk from St. John's Abbey four miles away and
editor of *Orate Fratres* (now *Worship*), did to rouse us to

a full sharing in the Mass. "At the Offertory you're up to bat. Don't be sleeping on the job!" he urged us. "Once you've put yourself on the paten, stay given. There must be no theft in the holocaust!" Everything he said was geared to our being live Christian laywomen. I knew he could tell me how I was supposed to know what God's will for me was. I made it clear that I felt no attraction at all for the religious life. It was a neat "I'm-not-the-type" statement. He took me at my word and didn't bother to tell me there is no "type." What he did say was simple and settling. "There will come a time when you'll know God's will by two signs: by a strong inner conviction and by external circumstances."

I knew that Father Godfrey was right. I went home to wait for the signs.

An army colonel for whom I had done secretarial work during two summers in the Military Attache section of G-2 had written that I might come back to the Munitions Building any time. But when I kept seeing the eager or bored or mischievous faces of high school classes I had loved in a week's practice teaching, I went to see Agnes Collins, director of a teacher-placement bureau at the National Catholic Welfare Conference Department of Education. She gave me the telephone numbers of two Washington parochial school principals. Just as I was leaving, she said, "Wait. Bruce Mohler needs a secretary. You're too young for the job but he's desperate." She took me to the Bureau of Immigration office on the fifth floor. Riding home on the streetcar that night, I knew — deep inside and from circumstances — that I had found my place. I knew God's will; I knew it would be easy to love it.

It was. I worked with people of heroic stature, laymen completely devoted to serving Christ in the immigrant. Into our office came a constant stream of visitors, people like the Portuguese sailor about to be deported for illegal residence, cut off from his wife and American-born children; like the Austrian professor-philosopher fleeing the Nazis, desperately in need of a permanent U. S. visa; the big Italian longshoreman for whom the longed-for American citizenship finally attained was cause for tears; the American Cardinal, whose yard-long passport pages needed visas for twenty countries; the endless groups of missionaries counting on us to secure passports, visas, and transportation to every part of the world.

Every day was alive with people — the Argentinian with paper in his shoes instead of socks, able to explain brilliantly why he didn't believe in working, able to weep like a child because the government wouldn't permit him to return to this country if he went home to see his dying mother; the Irishman Pat who had come on his brother Mike's passport, suddenly discovered to be Pat and not Mike when Mike himself arrived as Mike; the princely Archbishop Glennon; the charming publisher Frank Sheed, bravely crossing the Atlantic when it was dangerous to do so; the friendly Bishops who, eager to put office girls at their ease, kept their rings hidden until Mr. Mohler entered with an, "It's good to see you, Bishop!" Our cases were endless, varied, and often emergent. I had grown well acquainted with immigration procedure and legislation, and I was at home in the passport and visa offices of the State Department and the waiting rooms of foreign embassies. It was a good life, demanding and satisfying. Every day we had tangible evidence that we had helped people in critical need. Nothing would have pried me away from that office if it hadn't been for Dante and the streetcars.

Early in my N.C.W.C. days, Margaret Lynch, executive secretary of the National Council of Catholic Women, had invited me to go with her to an oblate meeting at St. Anselm's Priory. Father Thomas Verner Moore, the famous psychologist now a Carthusian, conducted the monthly meetings, giving a spiritual conference in the Priory chapel, pouring tea for us in the school afterward, finally leading us to nearby St. Gertrude's for a holy hour. Those monthly sessions and my own reading kept me in touch with the Rule of St. Benedict.

More and more it became clear that if one wanted to be absolutely certain of doing God's will, one needed someone guaranteed to be a spokesman for that will. One needed a superior.

For a while I thought my mother might do. We were great friends. She is holy and wise and would have done anything to help me. But we saw eye to eye, and I had no assurance that I was doing anyone's will but my own.

For a while I thought a husband was the answer. God would bless a wife who chose to do her husband's will. Every night as I walked from the bus stop through a three-block stretch of woods, I prayed hard for the man I would marry, asking God to prepare him, whoever he was, to help me do His will.

Wartime Washington was crowded, rushing, and weary. Especially between five and six in the evening was it crowded, rushing, and weary. I rode home beside it on the streetcars and buses. I looked into its eyes. I saw its tired faces, sensed its aching shoulders, shared its aching-from-standing-eight-miles-across-town feet. Often I heard its chatter. Suddenly relaxed after eight hours of intense stimulation, I was an easy victim to any powerful influence. The weariness and misery of the crowds that packed the aisle beside me entered into my whole system. The shallowness of what most of them had to say to one another was a real weight on me. I'm sure their lives were not really empty; I know now that God is terribly interested in their affairs, no matter how inconsequential their conversation seems to be. I'm sure, too, that there were great men and women, real saints, riding beside me. But those long rides, now inching, now swaying down Pennsylvania Avenue, were a constant reminder of the possibility of missing the real mark. I was seeing and hearing and smelling what had been an abstract truth in college classrooms. Many among those crowds did not even know that God's will exists, much less that it is the only real norm to which man needs to conform. It was obvious that most of them were not at peace, even with themselves.

Night after night as they unwittingly or apologetically pushed against me, they forced me back to Dante and the question I didn't want to consider: How can I be sure I'm doing God's will? I didn't want to consider it for two reasons. First, I wanted to remain content in my work. I had become a real part of the Bureau. I knew I was doing the job well. I realized I was working for the Church and that that should satisfy me. Second, I was beginning to fear I had a religious vocation.

I certainly didn't pray for it, nor did I thank God for it. I cried and felt very stupid when I told my mother about it. I did everything to talk myself out of it, even up to the time I was packing my trunk. By that time I had written to Mother Rosamond and returned the application blank to the scholasticate. But, I kept telling myself, I was still free. I had made no commitments. I didn't have to go. And then on the streetcars — "In His will is our peace." I did have to go. I knew from the sure inner conviction that only in a religious community could I be sure I was doing God's will. I knew from external circumstances too. I had finished paying college bills. I had helped Mother buy a house. There was nothing to hold me back except my own revulsion.

After two years I resigned from the Bureau of Immigration, drank my last cocktail on the Shoreham terrace, left my beloved family and the lovely house on Hillcrest Drive. I couldn't show a spark of enthusiasm, natural or supernatural, for the life I was choosing. I only knew that I had to choose it.

Once in the scholasticate here, I tried not to look as I pulled on the black stockings. My aspirant's uniform, beautifully pleated, trim with white collar and cuffs, hung beneath my coat and often clung to my cotton-stockinged legs. Delighted as I was to be at home at St. Benedict's, I found it hard to respond to the enthusiastic congratulations of the sisters.

Tremendous graces came to the rescue in a hurry. One came

in the words of a nun friend to whom I had confided my distaste for everything about convent life, at least, as I supposed it would be. She said simply, "God doesn't ask that we do His will with emotional enthusiasm. He only asks that we do it." That was simple enough.

Another came in the form of three divisions of freshman college English. It was easy to be enthusiastic about teaching beautiful girls who were eager to learn. Before long I didn't notice the black stockings and the uniforms. By Christmas time I had accepted the externals so completely that I couldn't understand why people on the trains stared at me. Those months as a postulant must have been flooded with grace, for when June came I knew that I was indeed a bride walking down the chapel aisle. I was eager to lean my curly hair toward the Bishop's scissors, and I kissed the blessed habit with real joy.

It was only in the novitiate that I discovered that this life must be an intense love affair and not simply a resignation to a necessity. I learned, too, that once religious vows are made, the simplest good act is transformed, lifted above the natural to a new plane of excellence. I began to see what the Lord meant by the hundredfold in this life. The joys (and griefs!) of community life opened up. After four years of high school teaching and a year away at college, I know that my very salvation depends on my being knit to my community. My whole concept of the religious life has broadened and deepened. When I made final vows in 1950, I was as eager and deeply happy as any bride could be. But my reason for being a nun has not changed.

Much as the community needs teachers, much as the Church needs sisters for every kind of work, I have still only one reason for being here. I know with absolute certitude that when I obey my religious superiors, I do the will of God. That means I am one with Him in the deepest, surest way possible. What I do and how I feel about it does not matter at all, really. My superiors are human and can make mistakes. But I can't possibly make a mistake by obeying them. I have the word of God and of His Church that it is so. As long as I obey, I do His will. And in the midst of great turmoil I have the peace Dante was talking about, the peace the streetcars drove me to seek.

GOD'S OWN CHOICE

SISTER M. BRENDAN, S.C.I.C.[1]

IT IS almost thirty years since I was given my vocation to religious life, and it is still a glad, wonderful thing to me. Why is it mine? Because of God's marvelous and strange choice in bestowing so much grace upon a very ordinary and not too promising scatter-brain who, even when she had outgrown her childhood, pre-ferred to race through fields with her dog or tear her dresses following her brothers wherever duty, desire, or daring took them. Ever so often, for years after I entered, I would find myself trying to realize that it was really I, the wild little tomboy whose ways so often caused concern to my mother, and merited the name of "Gypsy" from my less exacting father; that it was really I, walking down the convent corridor, with

[1] *Sister Mary Brendan was born in Shediac, New Brunswick, Canada. After several years of doubt and indecision, she entered the Sisters of Charity of the Immaculate Conception, Saint John, New Brunswick. She has contributed articles and book reviews to Catholic and secular periodicals, and her doctoral dissertation, "Children's Understanding of the Mass," has been published by the Catholic University Press, Washington, D. C. For almost twenty-five years Sister Brendan has been on the faculty of St. Vincent's Girls' High School, and she resides at the mother house of her community, St. Vincent's Convent, Cliff Street, Saint John, New Brunswick, Canada. The works of this congregation include teach-ing, nursing, Indian missions, caring for orphans and the aged, and other apostolic activities.*

my precious religious habit, a sister, chosen by God to be His — my probation years all over — and "they" hadn't sent me home after all!

Once accepting the mystery of God's choice, of His goodness in giving me so many graces, my vocation seems to follow a very ordinary course. I think the earliest desire to become a sister was probably a response to my mother's frequent speaking of her own sister, who was a Sister of Mercy in Colorado. One might quite often have found a tousle-headed little girl holding a small blue velvet album in grimy fists, while she tried to invest with life and animation the picture of a lovely young girl with beautiful earnest eyes (and queer mutton leg sleeves and a much befolded, widely extended skirt); when she had studied the album, if no one were about, she might drag a chair from the kitchen into the "sitting room" to stand on, and peer at another hanging picture of the same young lady, while trying to stretch imagination far enough to make her laugh or even run a bit. She "was beautiful," my Mother said, "so kind, so understanding, and so full of fun," and she had given her life to work for God.

At Christmas, holy cards would come for us from Sister Raphael; we knew she had no money, ever, to buy us presents, and that she could not keep many things we might send to her. That was my whole concept of a Vow of Poverty then. And she had to go wherever she was sent, and do whatever she was told to do. And that was Obedience. And of course, she couldn't get married, but that didn't make much difference anyway. She wrote a few times a year — or when there was any trouble such as death or sickness, and her letters meant so much to my mother! But they never told us many details; she was in a hospital in a mining town; I did not then know the significance of "Cripple Creek, Colorado." I used to get pillow-slips and a black cashmere shawl that was in Grandmother's trunk, and dress up like a nun, but the dog didn't like playing nun, so that never lasted too long. When my sister and I played with dolls, I was "Sister Agnes" and she was to send all her children to school to me. The dream never faded.

At ten years of age, I made my first Holy Communion and had my first real contact with sisters. I remember well the sister who had the "English-speaking children's class for catechism"; there were about ten of us, whereas, it seemed to me, there was a whole church full of French-speaking children. She was very kind and I loved her, awesomely, but I knew I could never look so sweet and holy, for my eyes were not blue. I was much embarrassed when my mother told her that I wanted to be a sister; I sensed the fact that neither of them took my intentions very seriously; I did not doubt them, however, and I don't think I ever did. I was fully convinced that I wanted to be a sister; I just had to wait to grow up.

As I approached teen years, my deportment and interests did not apparently impress either my family or my friends as being particularly cloister-inclined, so I grew a bit secretive about it. When I reached Grade XI, my sister, who had always been an angel guardian to the graceless young "Gypsy" of the family, went to Normal School, and I was left alone in high school. I didn't do anything very bad, but I certainly did not do anything very good; I was *not* studious. My mother had always cherished a dream that her two little girls might be trained by the sisters, but the distance of our country home from the convent school in town prohibited the realization of her desire in the earlier grades. Now, since, as she declared, I was "learning nothing but slang and idle habits," it seemed that the sisters would be particularly well fitted to tame down and curb this impulsive, romping girl into something of a young lady. And so, after dubious consulting of the family budget, I was to be sent to a boarding school not far from home, which was humble enough to be within our means and which yet had a rather good reputation for scholarship.

In so far as becoming a lady was concerned, the results

seemed doubtful. Apart from fits of homesickness, I really loved it, and tried very hard to work and do all that was expected of me; home reports were "golden"; but when I reached home in person, poor Mamma thought I was wilder than ever, while I just thought I was making up for lost time. However, it was here, at the Convent of Our Lady of the Sacred Heart, conducted by the Sisters of Charity of the Immaculate Conception, that the vocation which had been but a shadowy, far-off thing, became a definite, well-formed plan. Taking a business course, I planned to earn enough money to put myself through nurse's training; then I would be a nun. The two years spent in boarding school changed my outlook and strengthened me in character and in religious practice. Daily Mass and Holy Communion grew to be part of my life that I would never again want to be without.

I did not speak often of my plans, but the family knew what my decision was. However, only my sister really believed that it was more than a bit of infatuation that I would eventually outgrow. Mother, with rather conservative ideas as to what was befitting a maiden with such plans, at least pretended to be shocked at my enthusiasm for dancing and at the pleasure I took in arranging my hair. She used to look at me with a mixture of reproach, puzzlement, and loving pride as I dressed for a party, and with slightly baffled attempt at understanding, she would say, "Where is the little girl who is going to the convent?" She was not impressed when I'd laugh and kiss her, assuring her that God didn't mind my dancing and that I'd cut my hair off before I became a sister anyway. Sometimes she would talk very seriously, trying to make me realize that "there were two sides to everything," that I would not find "everyone in the convent perfect," that I'd find there people whom I could not like, just as I would anywhere else, and that I'd have to be very holy, for it would be better never to be a nun at all than not to be a good one.

Then came shadows. The war was nearly over, but my

brother was still overseas. The terrible flu of 1918 swept the country, wiping out whole families. My sister was very ill and had to spend several months in a sanitarium. My mother and I were left alone to take care of the farm, and that meant that I had to give up my office position and return home for six months. After this, my father's death and other changes left more and more responsibility on me, and my ambition to become a nurse began to grow dim. I had not made the pile of money I wanted and needed, and four years had passed. If I waited three more years while I took my nurse's training, who could assure me that at the end of that time I should still want to be a sister? With my lively fondness for fun, dancing, and being with the crowd, might I not meet someone who would change my mind? And I didn't want my mind changed. I started shaping more definite plans. I was working again, going to daily Mass during the winter months when I boarded in the city, missing it sorely during the summer when I lived at home, although I was always so happy to be at home.

I talked with confessors but did not receive very definite encouragement. Then one evening, Monsignor Savage, the pastor of the city parish in which I lived, gave a lecture in the parish hall on his trip to the South Seas and told us of the marvelous work being done there by missionary sisters. The next day I rang his doorbell and asked where I could get in touch with those sisters. When I had finished, his kindly face lighted up with a little smile, but he was very definite: "I don't think you'd like it. If you really want to be a sister, there's plenty to do around your own back door. Go down to the sisters in Saint John." Later, when he knew me better, he admitted that he had not believed me to be serious at all, just excited.

At that I decided to "go down to the sisters in Saint John." But now no one seemed to take me very seriously. The sisters at Sacred Heart Convent all knew me and thought I'd enter the convent, but why did everyone else to whom I confided my plans appear so skeptical? One priest told me, half in earnest, "to take six months' leave of absence from my job and buy a return ticket!"

I decided that I'd have to tell the Mother Superior just what I was like so that she'd know whether or not she could accept me. But sisters always understood girls, and it would not be hard to write to her. My letter might be described as a cross between a general confession and a class prophecy — and ended with a joke. (Surely any sister could take a joke!) "Even the ouija board says I'm to be married!" That joke nearly ended my chances with "the sisters in Saint John," for the reply to my letter was a not too warm invitation to "wait another year."

So another year I waited. Then I decided that I would wait no longer; if the Saint John sisters did not want me, I'd try other communities. My next letter was brief and to the point. I had waited, and now if Reverend Mother wished to give me a trial, I would prefer to enter with the sisters to whom I had gone to school; if not, I would apply to another congregation. The Holy Ghost must have been watching while life's ups and downs did the taming that the sisters had been unable to do. Sickness and death in the family had taught me much; responsibility and work had helped. I was still very lively and decidedly not the type that the neighbors could picture in the convent. But when the Mother General, in reply to my letter, invited me to visit her in Saint John, I put my head on my desk and cried for sheer joy.

Once it was settled that I should enter on September 8 of that year, I told people quite freely. I did not want them to think that I was suddenly diving into the convent with a broken heart — or any of the other idiotic things that my friends, especially the non-Catholics among them, were likely to think. I wanted them to see that I was just as happy and lively as ever and that religious life was a plan for living, not for dying out. In a word, I was going to the convent because the world had nothing half so good to offer me.

Not many thought I'd last long. One lad, a Baptist minister in the making, by the way, told me I'd do better in vaudeville than in a convent, and an old lady said she had always thought I'd make such a good farmer's wife. The whole family laughed that one out on me!

Was it hard? Yes. I must say that the last days were lonely ones, but sweetly warm and peaceful, too. It is strange what deep peace and happiness can dwell in a heart that is at the same time aching. For years I had offered the Fourth Station of the Way of the Cross for strength on the day when I'd have to say good-by to Mother and my dear ones — more for them than for myself, and I can truthfully say that God took care of it in the same way He takes care of all things we place in His keeping.

My days in the novitiate were happy, filled with eager desire and plans for the future, but at times homesickness hit with full force. Deep down I was always happy, but I could not help wishing for home. There were times when, were it not for deserting God, I would have rushed back. There was the time, for example, when I received a letter from home telling me that one of my brothers had been stricken with tuberculosis and had been sent to a sanitarium. I still vividly remember how mingled were my feelings as I took that letter to the Mistress of Novices, feelings of sorrow for my poor brother, of course, and for myself a half fear and a strange half hope that this would mean I could not go on. For if I could not continue because of something entirely beyond my own control, then I would not be refusing God. So often I had, ungratefully I know, found this cowardly attitude toward my vocation, both before entering and in the novitiate. And yet I knew deep in my heart that nothing could ever make me truly happy outside the convent, nothing else could ever bring out all that was in me or completely satisfy — nothing except the knowledge that I had given God what He wanted.

At Easter, when I took the holy habit, my mother came to be present at the ceremony. "One look into her eyes, and I'll know whether she's happy or not," she had assured the family, and if the look told her I was not, she would take me home with her. But the look must have been completely satisfactory. Mother came again for my First Profession, equally ready to step in if there were any indications of unhappiness. That seemed to end her doubts, and as the years went by, the family grew to value more the blessing God had given their "little black one," and to feel that there was strength for themselves in having their Sister Brendan so close to God.

Crosses there have been, as there must be in every life, but my religious life has always been full of blessings and happiness. I do not feel, as some outsiders have hinted, that I have been fortunate in having so many breaks in the monotony by attending university and so forth. It is true that many advantages have been offered me by my community, but I have been just as happy, in fact much happier, during weeks when I was teaching a classroom full of children or working in the laundry or in the kitchen. For religious life is rich and deeply satisfying in its graces, its companionship, and its closeness to God, and ultimately no outside interest can add anything to it. The roses have thorns, of course, and the cross of Christ must be borne even by religious, indeed especially by religious. Yet any activity undertaken under obedience and done as part of one's service to God can be very rewarding in happiness as well as in merit. One must be a cheerful giver, remembering that the joy of which St. Paul speaks is rooted in doing all for the glory of God.

THE GIRL FROM WAIKIKI

SISTER MARY MARGUERITE, P.V.M.I.[1]

"GOD is love, Lahela," my mother used to tell me in her soft Hawaiian way. Her words were punctuated by the sound of the breakers on the most beautiful beach in the world, the famous Waikiki Beach of Honolulu. Her eyes would seek the horizon and then look down into the small, upturned brown face which happened to be mine, as though she were seeking the God she spoke about. I think she found Him — she seemed to find Him everywhere.

For this is the traditional story of a missionary vocation in reverse. Not "American girl goes as missionary to South Seas," but "South Sea island girl goes as missionary to America"! From Lahela, my Hawaiian name, I have become Sister Mary Marguerite in a thoroughly American home mission community called the Parish Visitors of Mary Immaculate. And I think my mother's simple religion lesson, "God is love," had much to do with it.

The story begins in the best traditions of the fairy tale:

---

[1] *Sister Mary Marguerite came from her native Honolulu to the United States and became a member of the Parish Visitors of Mary Immaculate, whose mother house is at Marycrest, Monroe, New York. The work of the community includes parish census, family welfare, counseling, and catechetical instruction. Sister Mary Marguerite is herself engaged in home mission work and family counseling.*

brilliant, talented scion of a German-French family, settled in the Islands since whaling days, marries good and lovely Polynesian girl, and is promptly disowned in consequence. My father, Edward Voeller, was a sculptor. My mother, Anna Poepoe, was a full-blooded Polynesian, whose father had edited the first Hawaiian-language newspaper, translated the Bible into Hawaiian, and served in the House of Representatives. His wife was a lady-in-waiting, in her youth, to Queen Liliuo-kalani, the queen who in visiting Victoria of England remarked, "I too have English blood in my veins — my ancestors ate Captain Cook!"

After the marriage, my father, being disowned, was forced to work as a carpenter. So we were poor. My home was a bare, unpainted five-room house on the edge of Waikiki Beach, with the turquoise Pacific lapping and crashing at the outer edge. There was not much furniture, but there really wasn't room for much, once you got fifteen children, seven boys and eight girls, my father and mother, the two children my mother adopted because there was no one to care for them, and the assorted and constant flow of visitors, into the house.

But our poverty never weighed upon us. We spent our healthy, effervescently happy childhood days in swimming and rowing and laughing and fishing in the unending sunlight, and our evenings sitting with groups of neighbor children on the sea wall, singing and weaving flower leis. We went to school, of course, but largely because it was inflicted upon us.

The general tenor of life in the little house at Waikiki was "share and share alike," and when there was nothing to share, take it like a good soldier. My mother had good discipline; with a houseful like us, she needed it. Gentle and smiling as she habitually was, she said firmly, "I don't want to have to tell you anything twice," and she brooked no transgression of that law.

The only religion lesson she ever taught us was, "God is love," and she would continue, "and the way you show your love for Him is by the love you have for others. If someone starts a disturbance, say nothing to him. Just say to yourself, 'God is love,' and walk away." I think the reason I have never forgotten that lesson is that my mother came as near to living it twenty-four hours a day as it is humanly possible to do.

For formal religious instruction, she trusted the church-going which was mandatory in our house. At seven I was baptized in the Mormon Church, the religion of my parents, and called Rachel. We went to church on Sundays, and on Wednesdays to prayer meeting at one of the Hawaiian homes, where it was held in rotation.

But it was my mother's all-inclusive kindness, a love which embraced everyone and everything, which, together with her deep gratitude to God for the simplest things, were the major religious influences of my childhood. The night prayers she led often lasted, to our consternation, fifteen minutes, and her grace before meals, ten. She simply could not thank God often enough, or long enough, or sincerely enough to express the loving gratitude in her heart for the life and health and joy God had given us all.

There was school, one of the public schools of Honolulu. But until high school athletics came along, school was, as I have said, strictly in the category of a necessary evil, as far as I was concerned. Then I learned methods of instructing in athletics, captained the basketball and baseball teams for several years, and rowed in many island boat races. During my third high school year I was forced by the death of my father to leave school and go to work. (Later with the aid of an uncle, I finished school and studied at the University of Hawaii.) I had yet to learn that God sometimes uses the things we like to bring us to the things He likes, since it was my love of high school athletics which led me to the place where my slowly dawning restlessness would be forever quieted by the truth of the Catholic Church.

I found congenial employment as a dental assistant, and later as interviewer, in a settlement house called Palama Settlement, and was soon also given part-time work as instructor in six sports. It had been my childhood ambition to spend my life working for the poor, and now it seemed that that ambition had been fully satisfied. I should have been supremely happy, for my other love, music, was receiving its full share of attention, too.

Starting in the choir of the Mormon Church, I was soon singing Hawaiian songs at social gatherings, and then over the Honolulu radio on programs sponsored by various business firms. On Sunday evenings, I sang at the famous Honolulu Lau Yee Chai Chop Suey House. I loved to sing, to work for the poor, and to instruct in athletics. I was doing all three and in doing so, earning more money than I had dreamed of as a child. And still there was a void.

Just then, when I hoped to make my mother's life easier and more pleasant, she died suddenly of a cerebral hemorrhage, poor perhaps in money, but rich in love and confidence in God. After my mother's death, I was still active in the Mormon Church, especially in the choir, but it was beginning to seem a little empty to me, very much like going to a house where the mother is not at home.

Still, I was chosen to attend a young people's Mormon Convention in Salt Lake City, and accepted. We went to all the Mormon temples, met all the high officials of the Church, and learned Mormon beliefs and practices to the last detail, yet I returned to Hawaii more confused than enlightened. I was beginning to have vague misgivings about many of these beliefs and it puzzled me that the Mormons had a human founder, if theirs was a divine church.

I had not thought of the Catholic Church as even a remotely possible solution to my difficulties, until a friend invited me one evening to go with her to a triduum. She explained that I would only have to sit there while a priest preached on a religious subject and that I would not have to give to the collection! I went. The "religious subject" that evening turned out to be "hell"! I had given no thought to that place of eternal punishment, but Father Vaughan, S.J., from San Francisco, was very specific about it, and most impressive!

On the way out of church, my friend decided to go to confession. At the time, I thought the little doors along the wall led into closets. She murmured something about my waiting for her, but, not to be outdone, I went into one of the "closets," too. Seeing a priest sitting beyond a little screen, I told him I was not a Catholic but wanted to say how much I liked the sermon. The sound of his voice as he thanked me gave me strong suspicions that he was laughing. Such was my first initiation into things Catholic.

Not long afterward, a friend begged me to help out the sisters at a new Franciscan convent school in the lovely valley of Manoa; they had been unable to obtain an athletic instructor for their pupils. Very slowly and reluctantly I agreed to fill in, although my days were already full. The first afternoon I went to the school I met Sister Gonzaga, one of the teachers. She was calm and friendly and sweet, and looking not one bit like the instrument of divine grace she proved to be.

Our friendship grew, and I tried to tell her about my faith, but when I had told about the social events and the fund-raising meetings, there was no more to tell.

Occasionally, Sister invited me into the chapel. It was clean and beautiful. My interest grew, and one day six months later I said, "I am getting very curious. Will you please tell me something about your Church?"

My instruction had begun. It lasted six months, and little by little, Sister introduced me to the various doctrines, to our Lady, and to the saints. The thing I found hardest to accept was the Church's teaching on our Lady. Our Lady has taken sweet vengeance for that: she has become my dearest friend, has sent me to a community dedicated to her, where every sister bears and uses daily the name of Mary. Every day, now that I have found the house where the Mother — and her Divine Son — are eternally at home, I ask her to forgive me for those days when I did not know her, and thought that too much was being made of the Mother of God.

Sister's program of instruction introduced me to Catholic books, movies, and radio programs. Monsignor Fulton J. Sheen, now Bishop Sheen, was the one who cleared up my difficulties about our Blessed Mother by his beautiful sincerity in speaking of her. Since my baptism on July 11, 1940, I have never for an instant had a single doubt of any Catholic doctrine, and this I ascribe to Mary's protection alone.

From the day of my baptism I became a daily communicant, and thus became acquainted with the Maryknoll Sisters attached to my home parish. I was much honored to sing for their then Mother General, Mother Mary Joseph, and to receive from her an invitation to visit her, should I ever be in the United States.

Sister Gonzaga had entered religion young, and was thoroughly and completely and beautifully in love with her vocation. Naturally, therefore, she talked of it to me, of the wonder of God Himself actually inviting a girl to belong to Him alone, to serve Him alone, to love Him alone, and thus to become a saint, for His pleasure alone. It was as though I knew that some day God would want me to do just that, and I was frightened.

Almost at once I began to review to myself all the interests I already had, how busy and happy I was, how impossible, for me, was the religious life, how unnecessary, really. Besides, I argued, Sister Gonzaga and her like were lace-paper angels — being all dressed up in a habit and not being free to live one's own life were easy for them. But for *me*? Oh, no! Oh, *no!* I even said to her once, "Just because you are locked up here, there is no need for my being the same way!" Sister laughed at the "locked up" theory, and prayed, and went on loving her religious vocation — and talking about it. And I went on fighting mine.

But the seed was planted, and the memory of my mother's "God is love, Lahela," watered it. I am sure that my mother must have been praying for me in heaven. Mother had said, "The way to show our love for God is by our love for others." Try as I would to ignore it, the thought kept recurring, "How can we better show our love for Him than by giving our lives to serve Him, in others?" But I said nothing to anyone.

So I was thunderstruck when, one morning after Mass, Father Ferron, one of the parish priests, stopped me to remark, "I had a dream last night about you entering the convent."

I gulped, wished that the ground would open up and swallow me, and answered the last thing I had ever expected to say. "I hope, Father, that God will find me worthy to work for Him some day." And I realized that I meant it!

After writing to several communities (Sister Gonzaga did the inquiring for me), I narrowed it down to two, a Southern community and the Parish Visitors of Mary Immaculate, both engaged in family counseling, home missionary work, and the like. Deciding on the Southern community, I talked to the chaplain at the convent school, and he encouraged me greatly in my vocation. I determined to go over to the United States, and, if things worked out, to stay and enter that community. However, before entering the convent I would go to New London, Connecticut, first, to visit my sister, who was not well.

Arriving in New York, I registered at a midtown hotel, to rest before the last lap of the trip to New London. Sitting in my room, I looked through my address book, remembering the Maryknoll Mother General's invitation to visit her. If Maryknoll was near, I thought I might. I found instead the New York City address of the Parish Visitors of Mary Immacu-

late. There it was: 328 West 71st Street. That was only a few
blocks away; why not go and see them?

My heart was pounding hard with excitement when I met
the sister who was then Assistant Mother General. Sister
Mary Catherine was tall and gentle and very kind; I learned
later that she was one of the first members of the community,
a real pioneer in this work of family visitation.

Sister told me all about the work of the community —
that they contacted the Catholic families by means of a parish
census, directed by the pastor of the parish, and thus found
and reclaimed countless fallen-away Catholics. They brought
couples to the rectory for convalidation of civil or non-Catholic
marriages, instructed children for First Communion and con-
firmation, especially the public school children or children of
negligent families, notified the priest of aged shut-ins so that
they might receive the sacraments, and directed parish clubs
and sodalities. Sister talked of it all very matter-of-factly, and
ended by saying that some of their missions were exclusively
catechetical, teaching in catechetical centers for public school
children, and visiting their families, especially those with
spiritual problems.

I sat there and felt smaller and smaller — I who had so
many interests, I who had no use for being "locked up" as
a nun! These sisters were calmly, silently, unobtrusively doing
more for souls in a week than I had done so far in my lifetime.
Sister brought a postulant to the parlor so that I might see
how they dressed, while they were training. The dress was
long and black and slim and simple, and to my relief there
was not nearly so much serge as Sister Gonzaga had worn, and
while this was only a postulant's dress, Sister's habit was almost
as slender and simple, though of a different style.

Sister sent me to the community's mother house, called
Marycrest, at Monroe, New York, a beautiful town in the
mountains fifty miles northwest of New York City. When

I alighted from the taxi before a tall fieldstone mansion atop a hill, the portress, an aged nun, greeted me. I said, "I am from the Hawaiian Islands."

Sister's eyes widened in surprise. "And you speak English?" I was so stunned by the question that I was not sure for the moment whether I did or not. Then we both laughed, and she took me into the chapel, and I knew I had come home. The impression was confirmed by my interview with the foundress, Mother Mary Teresa Tallon. All the doubts and questions were smoothed away by this serene woman with the warm brown eyes and the clear, strong voice, and the decisive manner of speaking and acting.

I spent a sleepless night in the guest cottage, but by morning I had decided that here was where God wanted me, here with the Parish Visitors of Mary Immaculate, showing our Lord my love by serving Him in others in a way that so thoroughly suited my tastes, my temperament and my training — missionary visitation, family counseling, catechetical instruction. I could do good in the world, could even do part-time, and to some extent full-time, in the Hawaiian settlement work, the kind of service to the poor that I had always dreamed of doing. But it would be doing it *my* way, not *God's* way; it would be dividing myself, in a sense, and not giving Him quite all that I knew He wanted of me.

Slowly, since then, with the grace that God gives so generously and continuously to religious, a point which I had entirely overlooked has come home to me. It is the very important one that we can help others to know and love God only in proportion to our own love for Him, that we can influence and reclaim sinners, or anyone else for that matter, in exact proportion to our recollection and union with God, no more and no less. The life of prayer and contemplation is and necessarily must be the very life-breath of a mission such as ours.

I took my final vows as a Parish Visitor of Mary Immaculate

on the Feast of Our Lady's Visitation, July 2, 1948. The community's ceremony includes our offering of ourselves as "willing holocausts for the most abandoned souls," and the emblem we receive at final profession is an ebony and silver crucifix. Yet we are happy with that hundredfold joy and peace that, as our Lord Himself promised, only He can give. And if there are little hidden daily sacrifices of taste and inclination, as there are bound to be, it is these which provide us with the bulk of our "holocaust." After all, religious life is meant to be a *giving*, to our Lord and others, and not a *getting* — and we would not have it any other way.

THE BIRTH OF A DECISION

SISTER ST. HENRIETTA, C.N.D.[1]

"Helen, you're being influenced."

I understood well to whom my mother was referring.

"No, Mamma. I wanted to enter before I went to college."

Mamma looked at me for a long moment, then her eyes dropped. The silence grew harder till she finally spoke.

"Well, my dear, it is your life. I don't approve of what you want to do; but remember, you are our daughter, we'll give you everything you need. Go to bed, now."

With Papa it was different. I did not tell Papa; Mamma did, and I never learned just exactly how the interview proceeded. Papa was one of those Irishmen who will admit only two authorities, God and his wife. We were not too sure about God, but though Papa always came out best in an argument, Mother always won.

At any rate, Papa did not broach the subject and there began what might be called the period of Calm Disapproval.

This was not the first time Papa had disapproved of me. In fact, I started out life badly by being born the wrong sex.

---

[1] *Sister St. Henrietta was born in Montreal, Canada. On being graduated from Marguerite Bourgeoys College, she entered the Congregation of Notre Dame, whose mother house is at 3040 Sherbrooke Street West, Montreal. The members of this community are engaged in teaching on all levels and in missionary work in Japan. Sister St. Henrietta is a teacher in St. Mary's High School in Saint Albans, Vermont.*

One girl . . . , yes, Mother should have someone for company, but why two! He looked at the red-faced little bundle with the black hair and button nose and returned to his man's world of business. This disinterestedness led to our first open conflict.

About six months later Papa stopped for a fresh appraisal of his youngest daughter, found her better looking, and picked her up. I began to scream. He had not meant it to happen, but he was literally a stranger and I would have nothing to do with him.

Mother rescued both of us, but then and there the decision was made; something must be done. I might be a girl — that could not be helped now — but I was his daughter and he and I had better become acquainted. He was not going to concede approval, though. I should have been a boy, and "Boy" I was till he died. With that little gesture of nonconformity he set out to make friends, and did it so well that from that day to the day of my decision no major division had occurred. On the birth of my first niece Mother even overheard him telling my brother how much easier girls were to bring up than boys!

My childhood was a homely one in the good old-fashioned meaning of the word. By the time I appeared we were in comfortable circumstances but we lived plainly — more so, in fact, than most of our neighbors. I climbed trees, fought every boy and girl in the neighborhood, and collected broken glass. Mother had a strong hand which she used judiciously though sparingly. When Papa judged discipline advisable he turned me over his knee, grunted and stretched and adjusted to achieve a proper build-up, and then energetically slapped his left hand with his right — while I yelled lustily.

I was four when I started to accompany my sister to school. The following year I made my First Communion, and a year later I was confirmed. For the benefit of three old maids who conducted Saturday classes in the genteel art of fancy work I announced that I was going to be a nun. I was rather sorry that I was not a Protestant so that I could aspire to be a lady missionary like my best friend. A trip to the circus, however, revealed to me all the superior attractions of life as an acrobat, and I gave it serious consideration, though I never entirely relinquished my first idea.

As near as I can judge I was in my eighth year when I discovered *The Book*. It was Frances Hodgson Burnett's *Secret Garden*, which my sister had received as a prize. Once I had discovered it, it was no longer hers. I changed its life and it changed mine. I read the covers off the book and the type off the pages. Then I looked about for more.

My tastes have always been catholic. With complete abandonment to the book-of-the-moment, I turned from L. C. Meade to *David Copperfield;* from *John Halifax, Gentleman,* and Stevenson's *Suicide Club* to the Horatio Alger classics. I even sampled the Elsie books when nothing else presented itself — *anything* else was better. But the favorite of them all was, I must admit, contraband — *Nick Carter.* To you who belong to a younger generation I can only say that Dick Tracey, Hopalong Cassidy, even Perry Mason are pikers and sissies compared with that he-man who rode in and out of my literary horizon, scourge of wrongdoers and champion of the right. At least, that is the way I remember it. Perhaps, if I were to read him today I would find him overdone and insipid. It may be best to let him lie amid the glories of the past.

In the meantime I was growing up.

This was the era of the *Store*. Ours was a furniture store and it taught me many lessons of initiative, self-reliance, even self-abnegation. But it robbed me of some of my mother's comradeship, and I am not sure that I have ever completely forgiven it. Because my sister had brought home all the contagious diseases that visited our neighborhood and because I had left them strictly alone, she naturally had usurped a large part of my mother's time. When I was nine she went to boarding school, and Mother could have been all mine (except for

Papa and the older brothers, of course) but the Store stepped in.

Of course, I did not realize my loss then, nor do I, today, think I was to be pitied. I had a good home, a united, joyous one. We seldom entertained but we did love one another. My mother taught me to sew, to cook, and to take life as it came; my father taught me to say "No, sir," and "Yes, ma'am," to upholster furniture, and to play poker. I learned to smoke behind the shed, all by myself.

Our summers were spent on the farm in the country where we had a whole mountainside at our disposal and cousins to help us enjoy it. Some days we were even allowed to get the cows or help with the haying, a great privilege, indeed! It was then that my father made his greatest sacrifice, for he remained in the city alone.

But the Store, entering my life when it did, threw me to a large extent on my own resources. There was not the same chance for those little exchanges of small talk that are so meaningless and yet so revealing. Boarding school later only added to that intangible wall of reserve between my parents and me.

I have told all this because I am trying to trace the birth of my vocation. It was undoubtedly born at home, yet it came as a surprise to those who lived with me at home. We breathed religion but we seldom talked it. I have heard of other children being lined up for confession and Communion every Saturday and Sunday. *We* usually went with the other children from school. My mother and father often made the first Fridays, but no power on earth could get Papa to Communion twice on the same confession. His mother had warned him against that, and who was St. Pius X to contradict his mother! This remnant of Jansenism was not broken down till after I had become a religious, and then it was only by a priest who skillfully and tactfully suggested that perhaps his mother's heaven was being a little saddened because her son was following so exactly the advice she had given him.

Daily family prayer could find no place in our life as I graduated from baby forms to a more adult worship. Later when I was older and we had moved closer to the store, Mamma and Papa said the beads every evening during Lent, but they never insisted that I join them. They were too wise to ignore the past.

If I could point to one thing above all others that developed in me my vocation, it was the integrity which both my parents practiced and which they demanded of us. We were expected to be ourselves and to face ourselves without pretense or sham. Neither Mamma nor Papa hoped to make meticulous house-keepers of us, but life demands co-operation and we might as well get used to it. Hence we had our own "Share the Work" Program with mother as emcee and no prizes. Papa, as guest speaker, gave us lectures on the evils of piecework, pointing out that it encourages speed at the expense of quality. Except for a brief period, to prove his point, he never allowed it in the factory while he was in charge.

I hate to think of the consequences had my father ever detected in any of us a tendency to be ashamed of his origin — ship-fever Irish. He would have been angry and he would have been hurt beyond repair.

Teachers were not criticized at home. In general they were given a free hand. We were expected to take punishment as something a little less than we deserved — even if not at that moment. When intervention had to be made, it was done by my mother with a tactful assurance and with due regard for authority.

In view of these facts it may be wondered why I should have met with any opposition to my plans. The reasons were several. First, the idea came to both Mother and Father as a complete surprise. At that time, priests and nuns were a race apart, people who were to be respected highly but whose origins were unknown. There had been no priests in the family till my cousin had entered the seminary not long before, no sister till I made the break. Even our neighbors had been singularly unfruitful in religious vocations. It is not to be wondered at, then, that my decision should have seemed to be a heading for the unknown, a Kon-Tiki on the ocean of life.

Moreover, Papa had great plans for me. With the deep respect of the old Irish for learning, he kept all of us studying as long as we would co-operate. My own extracurricular work in college had led him to see in me a future great journalist. Was I not his daughter? And could he not supply me with an unlimited fund of (wholly unauthenticated) anecdotes? The prospect — if not the anecdotes — tempted me. I was also tempted to go on to a university and study mathematics. I liked clothes and even played with the idea of becoming a dress designer. My own wardrobe was being continually remodeled till Mother said in desperation: "Not again, Helen! I'll give you money for new material but *please* don't make that dress over again!"

Almost any career would have occasioned less bewilderment than the one I chose.

Many fingers were beckoning but one must make a decision, and I shall always believe that mine was made in my subconscious. My conscious mind just clung to it with the quiet resoluteness of my mother, or the defiant tenacity of my father — I have never been able to tell which.

There were other things, of course, which left their imprint. Not the least of these was the example and precept of my teachers, the Sisters of the Congregation of Notre Dame of Montreal, and the Religious of the Sacred Heart. With these latter I spent three happy years and I am sure that the daily rosary that I said in the chapel loft, as well as the way they made me work to be admitted as a Child of Mary (I made it a month before graduation), did much to focus my idealism. Daily Mass, of course, brought the grace and strength, but it is probable that the real and only answer to the wherefore of my vocation lies in the words of Christ Himself, "It is not you who have chosen Me, but I who have chosen you."

I did nothing to win Papa. We never discussed the subject except when the inner urge became too great and he exploded. Then my sister, Doris, would sometimes divert his ire in her direction while he recovered toward me his attitude of calm disapproval. It was best that way. All I could do was to let him see that I did not waver in my decision and, in my rare blue moments, to keep out of his way. I really believe that he respected in me the very thing that made him furious.

Papa did not say good-by to me. He had "to see a man about the church furnace" and left home before I did. I know now that he could not have endured seeing me go. With all the superb egotism of youth I did not realize that then. I might not have known my mother so well, either, had I not turned just as I went out the door. I had never seen my mother weep and she was standing by the door of the office, weeping.

Both my parents came to see me in the novitiate, and as the strangeness wore off, their attitude changed. The first definite indication I received was Papa's reaction to my new name. Mother was nicknamed "Hat," and when I told him that I was to be called Henrietta he put his arm around me and whispered, "Now I have two Hats!"

About Mother I was not so sure. Several years later, when she came to see me alone one day, I said teasingly, "I think you like Doris better than me."

Her answer was like herself, direct and terse, with neither dissimulation nor exaggeration, "Doris remained with me."

The matter was dropped and though the answer hurt deeply, I think we were closer to each other than we had ever been before. Mother had once again taught me a lesson. Had she been given to proverbs or platitudes she would have said, "You can't have your cake and eat it, too."

Doris had remained at home, and the love of a child for its parent had expanded and developed into the love of friendship. I had elected to travel along another road, and though the bond that united us was just as strong, its potentialities had remained undeveloped. Humanly speaking, the loss was great because my mother was someone worth being close to, but I do not regret it. The anticipation of a fuller knowledge and understanding has diffused in a human mist the over-powering and well-nigh incomprehensible radiance of heaven.

The change that took place in me was very different. I had aspired to become a religious because I believed that such was my vocation and I wanted to do something worth while for God. It was a reasoned thing but there undoubtedly were some moments of starry-eyed ecstasy. I was human, I was young, I was in love. Moreover,

> A certainty, a knowledge can be flame,
> Be sear, be burning in the soul to pulse
> In throbbed, repeated spread until the flamed
> Devouring moves along the last recesses
> And the soul is fire.

Stargazing is not encouraged in the novitiate; however, Woodrow Wilson once wrote:

"I believe that a man who tries to cultivate his character will cultivate nothing except what will make him objectionable and intolerable to his fellow men. . . . Character is a by-product. It comes, whether you will it or not, as a consequence of a life devoted to the nearest duty."

Reread that sentence substituting holiness for the word character, and you have an epitome of the religious life. Founders of religious orders knew it, and before they had finished with me I knew it.

One eventful morning I walked slowly up the aisle of the crowded chapel. It would be so easy to turn to the right, leave the procession, and be free: free to accept that fourth ticket my father had offered to buy for Europe and Carthage; free to make my mark in the world of wealth and fame; free to come and go as I pleased . . . not free, however, to do the one thing I wanted above all others to do.

The moment passed. With the others I stepped forward and advanced even into the sanctuary, there to vow my life to God. There were stars in my eyes then, I know, for they were the mirrored scintillations of the candle flame which symbolized my flickering, inconstant life, and the steady reflected glow of the silver cross which was earnest of God's love for me.

I placed my hands in His, and slowly and reverently I repeated the words which gave me life as they gave me death to self.

But it was Papa who had the last word!

It was the eve of my profession and the family had assembled for the signing of the contract which every novice makes with the community prior to pronouncing her vows.

The lawyer read the monotonous clauses of the contract and signatures were affixed to the impressive-looking document. During a lull in the proceedings, the family paused a moment to speak to Reverend Mother and her assistants who were assembled there. In the course of the conversation, Mother Assistant compared profession to a wedding.

Mother rejoined: "Yes, but we certainly were not overburdened with showers, trousseau, or reception. Just imagine the expenses *they* would entail."

But Papa, who up to this point had taken no part in the conversation, or for that matter, in my vocation except that of a bewildered and frustrated bystander, now felt it was time for him to take possession of the center of the stage.

Slowly he looked from one to the other of the V.I.P.'s assembled there.

"It's a mighty good thing it didn't take all that money. If they send her to Nova Scotia, it will take every cent I have to go to see her once a year."

There was a surprised gasp from the lawyer, an amused

chuckle from Mother Assistant General, a frown of incomprehension from Mother Bursar who had not grasped the import of the speech, and an annoyed glare from his youngest daughter. Only Mamma was unimpressed. After thirty-five years she knew her man.

Superior to it all, Papa folded his arms and leaned back with a gesture that said, more eloquently than words, "I have spoken; let the play go on."

SIGNPOSTS

SISTER MARY DAVID, S.C.[1]

I SAW my first signpost when I was eight years old. It was a dreary morning, and the second graders were shifting and coughing and casting side-long glances at the enticing rain. Just as Sister was beginning to consider it all a losing struggle, the door was flung open and a hearty voice, undampened by the weather, echoed through the room, "Good morning, Sister! May I come in?"

Without waiting to be encouraged, the priest strode in. Sister straightened her shoulders, smiled with resigned cordiality, and cast a warning eye upon the forty-nine who chorused their cheerful "Good morning, Father." At this moment Father seemed like an archangel delivering them in battle.

At the given signal they plunged back into their seats, and suddenly twenty-six boys were quiet and the bows on the top of twenty-three heads were perky with expectation. Father always asked questions, nice questions that any second grader worth his salt could answer. There were a few preliminaries and then the question of the day.

---

[1] *Sister Mary David is a Sister of Charity of St. Vincent de Paul of New York. She taught for a number of years at Cathedral High School, New York City, and is at present a faculty member of the Department of English in the College of Mount Saint Vincent. The Sisters of Charity of St. Vincent de Paul conduct orphanages, hospitals, and schools. The mother house of the congregation is at Mount Saint Vincent-on-the-Hudson, New York 71, N. Y.*

"I wonder what you boys are going to do when you're big. How many are going to be priests?"

Twenty-six hands leaped up, and as many pairs of solemn eyes looked into the face of the chuckling priest.

"Well, now, that's fine. And what about the girls?" He turned to us. "How many of you are going to be sisters?"

The girls did their best, and twenty-two hair ribbons quivered as the hands sped by them into the air.

A lone rebellious soul, I sat in the last seat of the third row, surveying the perfidy of my classmates. How could they, I seethed, how could they? And Sister, with the first real smile she gave that day — didn't she know? All the indignation at the command of a scowling eight-year-old flamed higher and higher — and then suddenly burned down into one determined resolution. I didn't care what the others said, I wasn't going to be a sister, and I wasn't going to say that I was.

Five years is a long time when it comes between the ages of eight and thirteen; but thirteen can suddenly be very wonderful. We had reached the seventh grade where a new seating plan was in effect. No longer were boys on one side of the room and girls on the other, but the boys and girls were alternated by seat and row so that, oh happy year, every girl was surrounded by four boys and every boy was surrounded by four girls. The boy in front of me discussed everything from the movie stars, whose pictures came on the inside of our ice-cream cups, to his spelling which, we both agreed, was terrible — and terribly important in the seventh grade.

Then one day we had a visitor. Since we had lost the fascination that "the babies" have for adults, we seldom had interruptions, and we were curious.

A brother's gentle old voice spoke of Christ's call, of the response to the call, of the generosity and love that impell a complete giving and a lifelong dedication.

It was frightening as he described it, frightening as can be a sudden glimpse into the blinding summer sun which leaves us blinking away the spots that dance before our eyes. The love of Christ, the call of Christ, the grace of Christ — it was a new world, known but unexplored until now.

And I knew only light, a brightness that defied words and left me consciously inarticulate.

I don't remember what happened immediately after Brother left, but as the whispered conversations continued with the boy in front of me they turned frequently to Brother, what he meant by this, what he said about that. Finally, from the seat in front came a question, urging and hesitant.

"Does a priest have to be good in spelling?"

I thought carefully before venturing a reply. It seemed to me that a priest had to be good in everything but surely, and this I said aloud, there must be some priests who aren't good spellers, and anyway he would pass spelling, I was sure. He didn't seem too certain, but he drew what comfort he could from my reply and we settled down to a discussion of the merits of religious versus secular priests. We didn't leave that topic for a long time, not even to talk about nuns — and I had no desire to, for now nuns were a part of a wonderful secret which I could share with no one. My feet hardly seemed to touch the ground when I walked, and my thoughts were riding white chargers along the King's highway.

But I was thirteen, and the riding was to be long before I should find my Grail.

I saw my next signpost during examination week in the eighth grade. Early every morning my brother and I raced to church, happily received Holy Communion, confident in doing so that all our examination troubles were over. One morning, toward the end of a successful week, a stranger caught up with us on the way home.

"What are you youngsters doing at Mass this week? I've seen you here every day."

We both chuckled, and then I said glibly, "We're having

examinations. We always come to Mass when we have examinations."

"Oh!" He looked at us. "Is that the only time you come?"

"First Fridays." I was less glib this time.

"I see," he said slowly, looking thoughtfully at us as he spoke. Then he smiled again. "Well, I hope you pass," he said as he lifted his hat; but before he turned on his way, his eyes searched our faces and we were uneasy.

We had little, almost nothing, to say to each other on the rest of the way home. In a moment our high spirits had been dashed, and as we paced along we felt cheap, very cheap. We had come for a gift; how often had we come for the Giver?

That signpost marked the turn of the road that led through four years of high school.

Our classes in high school started before the elementary classes, and so in the early mornings, I would gently close the door of my room, steal down the stairs into the foyer, and put on my hat and coat. The dark streets were uninviting, but Mass in the dimly-lighted, half-empty church was a blessed oasis. There was hardly light enough to let me read my prayer book, but after Holy Communion, there was occasionally a long time for thanksgiving.

Whenever I think of the origin of my vocation, I think of those Holy Communions; yet the thought of vocation preceded them, and the actual struggle to follow came long after. But there they lie, like diamonds in a wedding band, shining in the golden circle that begins and ends with God's love. I still did not know the how, the when, or even the exact why of what I wanted to do, but the realization was deepening that somehow I had to do it, and whether I wanted to or not was unimportant.

Reluctantly I would look at my watch, and if Mass had begun late, I finished my thanksgiving as I walked the lonely streets home. If I had awakened anyone that morning, I took the precaution of stopping at the bakery for a peace offering. But by the time I reached home, full daylight had banished Mother's fears, and my brother, as he breakfasted on freshly baked rolls, decided that I had the right idea.

An average teen-ager, I lived intensely in my own thoughts, and the growing realization of the goodness of my mother and father made the thought of leaving them almost unbearable. Their love had conceived its own dream and certainly it did not include the seclusion and separation of a convent. High school days were over, and with regret I began looking through college catalogs.

Once on Mount Saint Vincent campus, I was swept along in the full tide of college activities. And my eyes and ears were wide open. For the first time I met nuns on their own ground. Though the convent was strict cloister, the sisters and students shared the same chapel. We were never present at any of the community exercises except Sunday Mass, but gradually I was aware of the sound of distant bells, the prompt response of the nuns, the quiet joy and good-humored companionship.

Daily Mass continued and brought with it strengthening hope. Through sophomore and junior years I went every morning, knowing that He who demanded the sacrifice would provide the means of making it.

Then one Sunday morning at the community Mass, as I watched "the long black line" approaching the altar rail, the old, the middle-aged, the young sisters, the novices and the postulants, I realized the obvious. This action was the center of their day; nothing else, college classes, housework, friends, family, nothing else mattered ultimately — and in a flash a host of temptations assailed me. The vague and mysterious "world, flesh, and devil" of catechism days lost all their mystery as they started their warfare simultaneously on three fronts. Visions of highly mythical careers rose before me, and I played with them. Dreams of "good works in the world" held an inviting look, and the woman's craving for a family of her own became an insurgent and deadly foe. By the time of our annual retreat in junior year I was, in my own mind, dramatically comparing my struggles with those of St. Catherine of Siena, but even that little conceit did no good.

On the evening of the second day of the retreat (always a Waterloo) I broke the silence I was mildly endeavoring to keep, and told my problem, not to the retreat master, but to one of the sisters. It was a God-directed act, and she gave me a God-directed answer.

"Every vow is a sacrifice," she said. "Otherwise it wouldn't be worth making." And in exactly eleven words she vanquished the enemy.

Mid-terms of senior year brought a letter from my friend of the seventh grade. He was entering the seminary and he knew that I would be glad to know. Would I pray for him? I looked long at the letter and then re-read it carefully. Two words misspelled! Indeed I would pray.

At two o'clock one Wednesday afternoon a few days later I had no class, so I went to the small side chapel that opens onto the epistle side of the altar. The Blessed Sacrament was exposed and the sisters were in the main chapel saying the rosary, but I was alone. As I knelt, one thought kept recurring: Why did I want to enter the convent? Why did I want to become a Sister of Charity? I looked at the Blessed Sacrament searching for an answer that could be put into words, and the question was lost in the goodness of God's love. Now, too, I realized that my parents would never prevent my entering. The thought of their selflessness and generosity washed over me, and I was almost lost in the tide.

The tower clock struck three — I was late for my next class. But as I ran along the college corridor I knew that I was passing my last signpost and that soon I would be home.

Home! The struggles and doubts are long past and almost forgotten, and now I am one of the hundreds of "black cap"

Sisters of Charity who serve in the orphanages, hospitals, and schools of the Archdiocese of New York. Since 1817, when Mother Elizabeth Seton sent her first sisters back to her native city, they have found here their service to God in their service to their fellow men.

To be one of them, to share in their least service has been God's glorious choice for me — and I have an eternity in which to be grateful for the signposts that pointed the way.

A CENTURY PLANT VOCATION

SISTER VICTORIA FRANCIS[1]

JUST as God makes no two roses, no two birches, no two mountains exactly alike, so every vocation is unique. My vocation, for example, had to wait for so many years to come to fruition that I have often called it a century plant vocation.

It was described quite differently by my good friend, Monsignor William E. Cashin, ex-Sing Sing chaplain, who took great glee in identifying me as having gone "from crime to the convent." For five years before entering Maryknoll, I had worked only a stone's throw from St. Andrew's Church, New York City, where Monsignor was pastor. During these years he was a frequent visitor to my office when I was Case Supervisor in the New York State Division of Parole. After we had disposed of the immediate business of trying to work out parole plans for some Sing Sing protégé of his, we invariably talked

---

[1] *Sister Victoria Francis, a native of Fall River, Massachusetts, entered the teaching profession after being graduated from Smith College, and taught on both the high school and college levels. Later she embarked on a new career in the field of social service and spent several years doing pioneer work as Case Supervisor in the New York State Division of Parole. In 1935 she entered the Maryknoll Sisters, who devote themselves to the work of the foreign missions. Sister Victoria Francis is now stationed at the mother house of the community. The address is: The Maryknoll Sisters, Maryknoll, New York.*

about Maryknoll. In his Sing Sing days he had lived near the Maryknoll Seminary. He was at this time the Vicar for the Maryknoll Sisters and shared with countless others a deep respect and admiration for their foundress, Mother Mary Joseph. Monsignor knew that Mother Mary Joseph and I had been college friends. He did not know until I was about to resign the parole post in 1935 that I had been wanting to be at Maryknoll ever since the work of the Maryknoll Sisters began in 1912. These twenty-three years of waiting had been preceded by five years of growing interest in missions, so that all told my vocation was twenty-eight years agrowing.

This is how it began, way back in 1907, when our pioneer Catholic colleges for women had just come into being and were not too well known even among the clergy, so that when a Catholic young woman was interested in higher education she commonly attended one of the nonsectarian women's colleges. My choice of Smith College was based principally on the fact that St. Mary's Church was across the street. Among the one hundred Catholic girls at Smith College when I entered in 1904 was Mary Josephine Rogers of Jamaica Plain, Massachusetts, then a member of the Senior Class, whom we all called "Mollie." By the time I was a junior, Mollie Rogers had returned to the College holding a fellowship and serving as an instructor of biology. Early in 1907, all the Catholic girls received from her an invitation to form a Catholic Mission Study Class, the first such organized at Smith College where for many years the Protestant students had had numerous groups studying foreign missions.

About fifty girls responded. Mollie Rogers explained to us that she had been urged to form this class by Miss Elizabeth D. Hanscom, a devout Episcopalian, who was then faculty adviser on religious activities. She had then consulted with Father James A. Walsh, Director of the Propagation of the Faith in Boston, who had encouraged her to organize the class and promised to provide her with mission material. She warned us that this would all be in foreign languages as there was as yet no Catholic mission literature in English.

It was this class which opened up to me the vast field of Catholic mission endeavor through the centuries and filled me with hopes and plans to serve the mission cause. It was as a lay person that I first thought of serving, with Pauline Jaricot as a model.

When Father Walsh came from Boston to deliver a stereopticon lecture on modern mission martyrs, he introduced us to *The Field Afar,* the mission periodical he had just founded, and he appealed to the members of the class to volunteer to translate for its pages articles appearing in the European mission press. I was one of those who volunteered. For several years these bits of translation for *The Field Afar* helped to foster my growing interest in mission work.

Hopes for some American participation in foreign mission work rose when, in the spring of 1911 at the meeting of the Bishops of the United States, Cardinal Gibbons proposed the establishment of an American seminary for foreign missions. The immediate acceptance of the plan was a surprise. Father Walsh and Father Thomas F. Price of North Carolina were appointed to seek authorization for such a project from the Congregation of Propaganda Fide in Rome. The authorization was granted in Rome on the Feast of Sts. Peter and Paul, June 29, 1911. Maryknoll Seminary was opened the following September in temporary quarters at Hawthorne, New York, and was removed a year later to the present permanent location in a section of Ossining, which has come to be known as Maryknoll.

Meanwhile, on January 6, 1912, three young women began working first in Hawthorne and later at Maryknoll where, under the title of "Secretaries" they served as a "Pious Society of Women" established to assist the work of the Maryknoll Seminary. Their first work was to help in the editing and distributing of *The Field Afar.*

Wanting more than anything else to be one of the "Secretaries," who were the forerunners of the Maryknoll Sisters, I had to face the fact that I was not free to leave home. My father's prolonged illness had thrust upon me a major part of the responsibility for the maintenance of my parents and a maternal aunt who was also my godmother. In the beginning the "Secretaries" worked only as lay apostles and, as Mother Mary Joseph has written, "Few girls came to share such a life. The hope of being religious was unspoken and the expectation of doing work in the actual mission field seemed little more than a dream." When later the first steps were taken by Father Walsh toward forming a canonically recognized religious community, I must admit that this presented to me a new difficulty. I had always thought of myself as a lay helper. Up to this time I had not only felt no attraction but actually entertained considerable aversion to the religious life. I was rather grateful that present family obligations forestalled an immediate decision.

Despite all the variables of time and place, the essence of every religious vocation is the same. God sends His grace in the form of an invitation to serve Him in a special way. He shapes the circumstances of the call. To the man or woman who responds to such a vocation, its ultimate realization remains a mystery defying analysis or explanation. No Sister can explain *why* she became a nun. She can only relate the external circumstances which favored and those which hindered the fulfillment of her vocation.

At the outset there were for me two major obstacles: I was at first interested in serving the missions only as a lay apostle and felt some aversion to the religious life. Even if I were sure I wanted to be a religious, I was not free to leave home. God sent many helps during the struggle which continued over a long stretch of years.

For one intensely devoted to home and family and specially fond of children, marriage had much natural appeal. Marriage was, however, not any more feasible, because of my family obligations, than was a mission vocation.

When the Maryknoll "Secretaries" began their work in January, 1912, I was a graduate student at Smith College, having decided after three years of high school teaching in New England, to work for a master's degree. Obtaining the degree proved to be quite secondary in importance to the opportunities for spiritual development which the year provided. A mission given at St. Mary's Church by three zealous Vincentians focused attention on the then recent papal decree regarding frequent Communion. As a result of the mission I became a daily communicant. Only an adult who has gone through the experience of becoming such can have any concept of what this does to one's daily living.

The number of graduate students was small. One of the unusual subjects some of us studied was Gothic, the most ancient Germanic language. Parts of the New Testament are the only Gothic writings extant. The combination of daily Communion and daily study of the New Testament — even though it was only to translate it from Gothic into modern German — opened up to me a new way of living in which Christ seemed unbelievably close. The resulting sense of union with God began to be the all-important fact. There began at this time a new slow spiritual development that literally inched its way much like a century plant.

The repugnance which I had originally felt toward convent life was after a time transformed into an attraction so strong that I inwardly envied every sister I met. The first external help came from opportunities for close contacts with sisters which I had not previously had, particularly my association with the Franciscan Sisters at the College of St. Teresa in Winona, Minnesota, where I taught English from 1913 to 1916.

I next taught at the College of New Rochelle. The enrollment at the summer sessions was then divided about equally between sisters and laywomen. The religious included members of several communities. This was my first opportunity to see large numbers of sisters in different garbs mingling daily with women in lay dress — at Mass, in the classrooms, on the campus. There was borne in upon my aesthetic sense the realization that despite bizarre effects here and there the age-old religious habits had a beauty and a dignity against which the loveliest modern creation seemed to be shoddy. Once the old aversion to the way nuns dress was disposed of, the last vestige of resistance to convent life disappeared. My attraction to the religious life grew in intensity, and my desire to go to Maryknoll became so poignant by 1917 that, in order to cope with my inability to do so, I particularly needed the skillful guidance of a spiritual director.

This was ably provided by my Paulist friend and counselor over many years, Father John Marks Handly, who helped me to see that for a Christian the only matter of importance is to do God's will, and that His will is most readily found in the particular situation in which He places each one of us from moment to moment.

Accepting my filial obligation as my first duty, I came to see that I could nevertheless serve the missions by making everything I did every hour of the day an offering, a prayer for Maryknoll. This practice carried on, however imperfectly, through many years kept me close to Maryknoll in spirit.

Although I had up to this time enjoyed teaching, I had by now become convinced that I was better qualified to be a social worker, since my special interests, even as a teacher, had been focused on helping the individual, and particularly the pupil who presented problems. There was the question of securing training and experience. Night classes at the newly organized Fordham School of Social Work gave me my first introduction to what was soon to be my new profession. An opportunity to pioneer in the field of Catholic Charities came through my friend, Marguerite T. Boylan, who for over a year had been working singlehanded as the Executive Secretary of the newly founded Catholic Charitable Bureau in Bridgeport, Connecticut. Miss Boylan and I were associated in this work in the Hartford diocese for about twelve years. During this period a central office in Hartford and five other branch offices were organized to carry on casework with families and children. The Connecticut Council of Catholic Women was organized in 1920. By 1930 it had grown to a membership of 16,000. It was a treasured privilege to have a small part in this flowering of Catholic Social Welfare in Connecticut. My family and friends assumed that I found complete satisfaction in this professional career. Unquestionably there was satisfaction in serving people in need and in trouble, but actually all this social work provided satisfaction only as a substitute for Maryknoll and only to the degree in which I could every day make it a consecrated service offered up for Maryknoll.

In 1930 I left Connecticut and went with my father to New York City, my mother and aunt having both died in 1924. After a brief experience at the New York Foundling Hospital, there came an opportunity to serve as Case Supervisor in the newly established New York State Division of Parole, which according to recent laws was to be operated on the principles of social casework. This was to be a unique venture. No other state had made such an attempt. It was a stupendous task. The Division suddenly took over legal responsibility for approximately 6000 paroled felony offenders, about half of whom were in the metropolitan area. It was necessary to develop a system of parole supervision that would both safeguard the security of the general public and offer to paroled prisoners an opportunity for rehabilitation with the help of social casework.

The parolees being 98 per cent men, the parole officers had to be practically all men. Men with professional social work training were not available in sufficient numbers to fill the first posts as parole officers. Someone had to provide the staff with some training in social casework. Men qualified to be case supervisors did not seem to be available at all. It fell to me to set up a plan of in-service training for the large staff of men in the New York office, on which training in the other offices would be patterned. Later, when new parole officers were appointed, professional training was required. When additional case supervisors were appointed, they were men. It was in this man's world that I had lived and worked for five and a half years before finally entering the convent.

The final step began with the death of my father on September 9, 1934. For several years I had been convinced that I was already too old to be accepted by any religious community. I had begun to think that God, after all, had not intended me to be a Maryknoll Sister. But the desire to serve the missions still persisted. Unable to give direct service, I concluded that the only way God intended me to help was through the continued offering of my daily works and prayers for Maryknoll. Always finding it hard to save money, I remember that once, when a friend remarked that I'd better be careful or I'd land in a county home, my immediate thought — unexpressed, of course — was that, if this should happen, it would be something to offer up for Maryknoll. Several years were passed thus in this intellectual acceptance of the fact that I could not fulfill my desire to be a Maryknoll Sister.

Some deep force, of which I had been unaware, suddenly came forth with overwhelming power the very moment my father breathed his last. It surged through my whole being. "Now I can go to Maryknoll," repeated itself in my mind over and over again, as I busied myself with all the details of the funeral arrangements. The funeral over, I tried to reason with myself, fearing that this was just an emotional reaction and thinking that I was undoubtedly too old for acceptance by a religious community. To make sure it was not a passing whim, I waited until January before writing to Mother Mary Joseph, who I learned was away on a visitation. The Vicaress wrote me a discouraging note about late vocations. It was June before Mother Mary Joseph consented to my making formal application and then only after I assured her that I could secure a leave of absence from my parole post.

No end of minor difficulties occurred during the process of assembling the necessary documents. My baptismal record could not be obtained from the church because the records for that year had been destroyed by fire. A search for the family copy meant going through five trunks. It was found under the brown paper which covered the bottom of the fifth and last trunk opened. My birth certificate was almost unrecognizable, my father's surname and my mother's maiden name both misspelled and even the date, March 1, incorrectly recorded as May 1, while my baptismal certificate recorded my baptism on March 3 of the same year!

It was September 1 before I was accepted. I entered Maryknoll on December 7, 1935, to live through two and one-half years of novitiate training which were in many ways the happiest of my life. Because of my age, I had no expectation of being sent to the missions. I thought Mother Mary Joseph would just have to find something for me to do at the mother house. It never entered my mind that I would ever again do any active social service work. I did not realize what surprises the religious life can provide.

During eight years at the mother house I taught sociology in Maryknoll Teachers' College. My old interest in journalism found expression in working in the publicity branch of our mission education program. A tremendous surprise came in 1943, when I was assigned to Hawaii to pioneer once more. This time it was to develop under the direction of Most Reverend James J. Sweeney, Bishop of Honolulu, and Reverend Hubert P. Winthagen, SS.CC., Director of Charities, a diocesan Catholic social service agency with a staff of Maryknoll Sister caseworkers. In 1950 I was transferred to San Francisco for similar work. As a result of our 1952 General Chapter I am now back at the mother house.

Each day finds me more puzzled as to why the dear Lord should have wanted to work out such an elaborate pattern of circumstances to make me at last a Maryknoll Sister. Each day I realize a little more deeply that I did not choose Him, He chose me. Why, I do not know, except that once in a while, He chooses to grow a convent century plant.